MARGO ROUARD-SNOWMAN

330 ILLUSTRATIONS 179 IN COLOUR

museum
museum
museum

GRAPHICS

THAMES AND HUDSON

To my parents,
Odette and Edmond Rouard.

I wish to thank particularly Pierre Bernard,
Dominique Bozo, Roman Cieslewicz, Nicholas
Snowman and Jean Widmer for their support
and suggestions.

I wish also to thank Marie-France Monstin for
her valuable collaboration.

I am also grateful to Sido Hennequart and
Myriam Provoost, as well as all the designers
and organizations who have supplied material.

Preface and introduction translated from the French by
Alison Hollingsworth. Commentaries translated from
the French by Elizabeth Pendleton and Paul Collins.

Typeset in Monophoto Frutiger.
Printed and bound in Singapore.

Contents

GERMANY

ITALY

JAPAN

THE NETHERLANDS

SPAIN

SWITZERLAND

UNITED KINGDOM

Preface
Graphics for museums: an overview

This work is a collection of high-quality graphics, commissioned by art institutions and for events – museums, galleries, festivals and temporary exhibitions – all over the world. The term 'art' is used in the widest sense to include disciplines – architecture, photography, design and cinema – which have not always been accorded full status as 'art' by the museum world. This collection is neither, at one extreme, a coffee-table book, nor is it an extended portfolio. It is intended to be a reference volume full of information, where those who commission graphics will find a wide range of models and where those who design them may seek inspiration. It aims to present a balanced and comprehensive view of tradition and innovation in the field and is illustrated with a great variety of international examples.

The introduction first of all examines the recent proliferation of museums. There follow a brief history of art and graphics; a consideration of graphics and national identity; a description of the graphic artist's profession and methodology; a glance towards the future; and a select glossary of technical terms. After these sections come fifty-nine fully illustrated case studies, organized solely according to geographical location.

Since there is a continuous increase in the number and variety of graphic projects for the arts, this publication, which takes the early 1980s as its starting point, is by no means exhaustive. Any book simply casts light upon its subject and provides one particular view of the works which it has gathered together. Without this element of subjectivity, *Museum Graphics* would not exist in its present form, contributing as it does to the recognition of much professional talent.

Introduction
The museum boom

The museum, which first appeared in eighteenth-century Europe and America, has changed considerably over the last few years. Once poorly managed institutions, they have now emerged from a process of refinement, convinced of the need for a public image, or at the very least for strong posters, and have won for themselves a prestigious position. It is the museum and its temporary exhibitions that authenticate and exalt the fine and applied arts that make up their displays. Whether in the field of painting, sculpture, decorative arts, architecture, photography, design or cinema, the museum conserves its collections and interprets them for its visitors.

Twenty or thirty years ago, museums and the so-called 'cultural' enterprises had a reputation for elitism. This was due, among other things, to the difficulties of public access and to the conservative policies of curators, who were more concerned with acquiring rare pieces and with pursuing their own lines of research than with putting their treasures on show and introducing them to the public. Today museums and cultural events are regarded with respect. The public has a wide variety of attractions to choose from and is prepared to queue for hours to gain entrance. This boom can be observed just about everywhere in the world. Art exhibitions are becoming major events for which commissions are sought from architects, designers and graphic artists. Whereas it formerly opposed popularization, the art world is now witnessing museum marketing programmes which are doing away with the traditional barriers and creating professional opportunities for graphic artists.

The discrepancy which exists between the substantial investment granted to architecture and its leading lights, in what amounts to a 'star system', and the small sums allocated to visual communications is regrettable. On occasions, the poor quality of a collection is concealed by commissioning the building from one of the big names of international architecture. In such a case, the communications strategy is centred for the most part around the name of the architect and the building, to the detriment of a true policy of graphic communication. There is, moreover, another important aspect to this practice: the expensive 'stars' have to serve the interests of their employers. Consequently, they appear in every 'modern' and 'intelligent' electoral manifesto.

In France in 1989, for instance, 120 building projects were in progress, 70 of them large-scale programmes. In Paris, there is Ieoh Ming Pei's Pyramide and the Grand Louvre project; in Clermont-Ferrand, Adrien Fainsilber and Claude Gaillard's conversion of a barracks in order to house the Musée des Beaux Arts (cost: 50 million francs). In Nîmes, there is Norman Foster's Médiathèque (cost: 270 million francs).

This trend is not confined to France. In Germany, the major cities and *Länder* rival one another in their museum development programmes. Mönchengladbach commissioned a municipal museum from Hans Hollein (1972–82). Stuttgart commissioned James Stirling and Michael Wilford for its Neue Staatsgalerie (1977–84), while Ulm turned to Richard Meier for an exhibition and conference centre (1986–). Cologne built a complex to house the Ludwig collection, designed by the architects Peter Busmann and Godfrid Haberer (1975–86). In the democratic post-Franco era, Spain is in the process of renovating and enlarging the Prado; creating the Centro de Arte Reina Sofia (based on the Pompidou Centre); accommodating the Thyssen collection from Switzerland at great expense; and inaugurating the Fundació Tàpies (Roser Amadó and Lluís Domènech). In London, the Tate Gallery was the first to construct an extension to its existing building, commissioning the architects James Stirling and Michael Wilford (1980–85). The more traditional National Gallery followed suit with a commission by the architects Robert Venturi and Denise Scott-Brown (opened 1991). In Italy, the Palazzo Grassi in Venice has been restored by Gae Aulenti and Antonio Foscari in order to create a centre for contemporary art financed wholly by the Fiat group. In addition, there is the multi-media centre for contemporary art in Palermo designed by Mario Botta (1988–). In Japan, the Municipal Museum of Art in Kitakyushu was designed by the architect Arata Isozaki (1972–74). There is also the National Museum of Modern Art in Kyoto by Fumihiko Maki (1986), the Museum of Modern Art in Nagoya by Kisho Kurokawa and, as early as 1950, the National Museum of Western Art in Tokyo designed by Le Corbusier. In the United States, the museum for the Menil Collection in Houston, Texas, was designed by Renzo Piano (1981–83). The Guggenheim Museum in New York is adding to its existing buildings, with designs by Charles Gwathmey and Robert Siegel.

This flourishing of the museum world is closely related to the operations of the art market and contributes to an increase in both values and prices. Because the new exhibition spaces have to be filled, rare objects have to be hunted down and purchased. It is equally necessary to find sponsors who are willing to finance both acquisitions and conservation, and also to make exhibition spaces pay their way by attracting the general public. There is, therefore, a greater need than ever for professional graphics, not only for the purposes of communication, but also to attract a wider audience. Whether for reasons of taste, profit or prestige, private companies are beginning to finance cultural activities, thus relieving the state and local authorities of part of their burden. However, the real reasons behind this capital outlay must be considered, and the results must be clearly identified. For this reason there is a need for regular communication between institutions and their publics. At times the difficulty lies in maintaining a balance

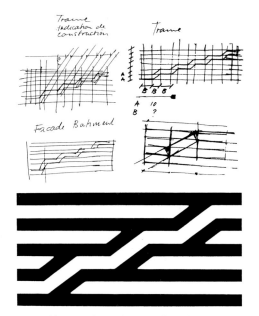

Jean Widmer and Ernst Hiestand's preliminary sketches and logo for the Centre Georges Pompidou (1974).

between financiers on the one hand and the integrity of artistic practice on the other. Graphic art can serve the launch of these institutions and events, but it must also enable them to communicate regularly with their different publics; to win the loyalty of their visitors; to confirm their national and international reputations; and possibly to gain an advantage over their competitors.

Unfortunately, it is rare to find a cultural institution which brings both enthusiasm and continuity to a visual identity programme. Often the museum curator regards with scorn the notion of a graphic identity for art and museums and persists in opposing a structured communications programme. In addition, investment in building often results in the neglect of graphics. International competition stimulates the promotion of the museum, while over the last decade, the benefits brought as part of this process to these temples of culture by the graphic arts can be clearly observed. As the art historian André Chastel commented in 1989, 'The museum must from now on be classified in the category of entertainment, and as consumer art.'

A brief history of graphics

DE STIJL

Vilmos Huszár's logo for *De Stijl* (1917).
***Below*: poster to announce the Pushpin Group's office move (1980; illustration and design by Seymour Chwast).**

Graphics is a recent subject based on the well-established tradition of typography which dates back to the fifteenth century and Gutenburg. Until the end of the nineteenth century, the development of printing was centred around the production of books and periodicals. In 1917, De Stijl began life as a magazine, its logo (designed by Vilmos Huszár) made up of letters drawn using basic rectangular shapes. In 1920, graphic artists broke with the decorative arts tradition, evidence of the strong and lasting influence of the Russian Constructivists. In the post-war period, graphic art began to mediate between the interests of institutions and the international economy on the one hand and a public of passive consumers on the other. A pioneer with regard to museum identity is the Stedelijk Museum in Amsterdam where, between 1945 and 1963, Willem Sandberg, the museum director, designed posters and catalogues.

In the 1950s, the Swiss schools came to the fore, becoming an international point of reference. This is the era of clarity, severity and of the systematic integration of text and image. The chief exponents were Max Bill, Otto Treumann and Joseph Müller Brockmann. In the Netherlands during the same period, Wim Crouwel's work anticipated 'objective design'. He regarded design as the solution to every problem. His graphic responses are structured and totally lacking in artistic pretension. He rejects all pictural and anecdotal images. An identical development can be observed in the plastic arts with the emergence of minimalist art and the 'zero movement'.

In the 1960s, a world order was advocated in which each individual is regarded as a potential artist. In the United States, the Pushpin Group took its inspiration from art history, while popular culture used humour and parody to confront modernist ideas. Pushpin played an important role in the development of visual communications in an international context, and it was at this time that the graphic design profession organized itself on an international scale. In 1963, ICOGRADA, the International Council of Graphic Design Associations, was founded. Almost everywhere there was conflict with the established order which resulted in the production of alternative graphics characterized by hand-drawn, highly plastic and anti-functional images. These graphics were at times difficult to read.

With the 1970s came the apogee of advertising and the first shy attempts by museums to develop a visual identity. In 1966, the Stedelijk Museum set up a structured

Stedelijk Museum: front cover of a 1957 catalogue (Willem Sandberg) and poster for a 1968 exhibition (Wim Crouwel/Total Design).

programme, designed and carried out by Wim Crouwel and Total Design, which continued and developed the graphic design strategy started by Willem Sandberg. The museum used a standard grid for all its catalogues and posters, thus conferring upon all its products, whatever their nature, a wholly recognizable graphic identity. An opposing view was held by Jan van Toorn, a graphic designer at the Van Abbe Museum, also in the Netherlands. He argued that a provocative graphics policy, based on 'stimulating the outrageous in order to awaken consciousness', is more effective. He rejected a uniform approach which 'conditions desires rather than informing or communicating'. These ideas were the subject of a public debate in November 1972, a debate which is central to the history of graphic design and which remains current today: the questions of rigour and legibility, and of free-hand drawing and confusion.

The expression 'visual communication' was coined in the United States in 1966 to cover various areas: typography, posters, layout, illustration, logo creation and so on. In 1977, the Centre Georges Pompidou opened in Paris, projecting a high quality visual identity created by Jean Widmer. The rapid development of visual communication in the arts and in local communities can be linked to the acceptance, characteristic of the 1970s, that there are certain virtues in advertising.

The 1980s was a decade of rapid change, when the cultural values of different countries became superimposed upon those of others around the world. This process acted as a counterweight to those stereotypes which are seen as embodying the national or historic characteristics of our cultures. The museum boom of the '80s, which was fed in part by this weakening of international barriers, had the effect of opening up the professional market to a great variety of graphic projects.

The 1990s are witnessing a growing tendency to theorize the profession of the graphic designer, which wavers between that of intellectual and artist. In addition, art institutions are now beginning to define and manage more comprehensive visual identification strategies.

Graphics and national identity

The works presented in this book cover a wide range of categories, including posters, catalogues, invitations, sign systems, publicity brochures and other related products. Graphics from the USA, Australia, France, Germany, Italy, Japan, the Netherlands, Spain, Switzerland and the United Kingdom, created over the last decade, have been selected for their professional excellence and their aptness to the user's aims. Overall, the evidence of national characteristics cannot be denied. Each creation expresses a sensibility inherent in the spirit of that country, and therefore appropriate to the promotion of that nation's artistic and cultural programmes.

In the USA, graphic design has no obvious orientation in any one direction. Instead, the diversity of modes of expression guarantees that all typographical trends are represented. A concern for the effectiveness of the graphic image, coupled with the financial involvement of companies in art institutions, means that highly apposite images are produced, although at times these lack refinement.

In Australia, graphic design is characterized by a variety of styles and freedom of expression which reveal the impact on graphic designers of different schools and trends. The work produced by the Australians is full of vitality.

In France, the use of images has traditionally played a more important role than typography. Different trends generate a variety of styles, which give ample room to

Poster by Günter Ranbow (1988) to illustrate the theme that knowledge alone does not create art.

expression through free-hand drawing and to a profusion of ideas deriving from various artistic influences: at times the result exhibits a certain degree of impudence. Since the state controls the country's cultural bodies, and since museums are the generating force behind art and media ideology, visual identity systems for museums are sometimes commissioned to stimulate creativity and to set valuable examples. As a result of this a market for graphics is opening up in a society where graphic designers still have difficulty in gaining recognition outside the world of advertising.

In Germany, the traditional use of images and typography is based on functionalism. This results in a rigorous adherence to the rules laid out in design standards manuals and leads to continuity in the use of high-quality brand images.

In Italy, the revenge of the amateur against cultural elitism, a sense of good taste and a respect for typography have all given rise to extremely free graphic creations which are wholly without academicism in their use of illustrations. Nevertheless, the home of contemporary design and the centre of pilgrimage for art lovers flocking to its great museums seems to be more prolific in the creation of household objects than in the production of graphic images.

In Japan, the concept of the museum is relatively new. Shuji Takashina, a professor at the university of Tokyo, says of the museum, 'It is an institution not yet a century old which has been imported from the West.' According to Professor Takashina, Japanese private collections belonging to aristocrats or to religious orders were not traditionally shown to the public, except on special occasions such as festivals, anniversaries and tea ceremonies. Indeed, the fragility of Japanese works of art, such as lacquerware and silks, prohibits their prolonged display. Recent museums are centred around Western art, but these venerable institutions have not commissioned visual identities. The fashion for temporary exhibitions has generated the publishing of many posters, sometimes of high quality, but lacking related visual supports in any other form. Major graphic designers, such as Yusaku Kamekura and Ikko Tanaka, produce posters in abundance, but have not always created graphic images linked to the art world.

In the Netherlands, graphic art is never regarded as a derivative art form. Dutch graphic culture and typography is unrivalled anywhere. Resolutely modern, open to all fields of influence, creative and abstract, it is regarded as being on an equal footing with other art forms. Outside the art world, one only need mention the Dutch Post Office which, since 1930, has employed professional graphic designers. The Post Office's policy is motivated by a certain freedom of action and creativity, a strong typographic tradition, a desire to promote graphics and to encourage letter writing. The Dutch authorities are a source of numerous commissions and their actions have a knock-on effect in that private companies are prompted to emulate them. Their tradition of non-decorative abstraction would seem to give the Netherlands a position of undeniable leadership in the field of European graphic design.

In Spain, political repression, which continued until the end of Franco's rule in 1975, made unlimited freedom of expression impossible. A few pioneers, such as Peret, have emerged, but they have so far received few commissions from the art world. The latter is recovering its identity, but without recourse to graphic design.

In Switzerland, graphic designers were responsible for the creation of a set of rules to ensure that information is legible and organized clearly, and that rhetorical devices are rejected in favour of honesty and the communication of information. The use of functional typefaces and of standard layouts for all documents ensures that

Poster by the Japanese designer Takenobu Igarashi for the University of California, Los Angeles.

Persbericht

The cloud-motif logo of Witte de With, Center for Contemporary Art, Rotterdam, as adapted for press release notepaper. (Gerard Hadders, 1989)

publications, whatever their nature, have a graphic identity which is wholly unmistakable in terms of the rigour of its design and its legibility. The rules which are applied exclude neither creativity nor the need for high quality, both of typography and illustration, and they give rise to excellent functional images. Whether poetry or parody, the overall effect of the visual images is in keeping with both the austerity of the typography and the modular construction of the layout. Legibility is always of the highest standard. Swiss graphic designers have gained a considerable following and since 1950 have trained numerous graphic design professionals whose methods are undisputed all over the world.

In the United Kingdom, there is a strong typographic tradition which gives a high priority to information and its presentation in a graphic form. Influenced by the punk movement and by the numerous magazines designed by Neville Brody (*The Face*, *Arena* and *City Limits*), graphic productions tend to harmonize type styles by creating word-images, while occasionally having recourse to illustration. The mixture of neo-classical and post-modern influences is bringing about a return to functional typography, while thanks to an injection of humour and surrealism, British graphic design is characterized by a number of singular styles.

Beyond styles and fashions, all the examples chosen for this book have one thing in common: quality. A number of different trends can, however, be isolated, each adapted differently according to national and cultural identities.

The influence of the Apple Mac computer can be seen in curved and twisted lettering and in ever-increasing combinations of different typefaces on the same item. If, however, the concept behind the graphic design is weak, then the computer-assisted end product becomes banal. The Macintosh can be used as a graphic tool, just like a pencil, and this has led to the appearance of hybrid images and to the creation of a new vocabulary.

One can also identify the trend of experimental typography, an intellectual approach which fragments the text in the space available and which emphasizes the aesthetic quality of the layout rather than the physical quality of the letter.

Fewer and fewer letters are drawn by hand.

Also identifiable is a trend whereby the text and the image are mixed in an ever more complex manner: the text is either superimposed on the image, or fragmented within the image, and so on.

Finally, there is the use of certain 'retro' typographical effects. These do not cause problems of legibility and create a very individual visual identity.

The profession of the graphic artist

Graphic designers are professionals, working either independently, or in small teams, or as part of a larger office. This might be in the in-house graphics department of an industrial design company or public body or in an advertising agency. Designers occasionally work for agencies which specialize solely in the creation of brand names.

Regardless of the size of the group within which a graphic designer operates, the difficulties presented by a communications project are substantial. His or her first task is to identify the communications needs of the institution which has commissioned the project and to provide an appropriate visual solution. The proposed response is composed of a variety of elements, such as type style, calligraphy, layout, choice of

Detail of cover by Jean-Michel Folon for the London magazine *Design* (1969).

media, paper, colours and the possible use of photographs or illustrations. The graphic designer is both an artist and a technician, tailoring his or her response according to the particular nature of the problem. As a mediator between the commissioning institution and the public, he or she contributes to the successful promotion, or otherwise, of the subject. In their work, graphic designers exploit and develop the range of areas where their expertise is needed: visual or corporate identities; advertising campaigns; published material such as posters, brochures, catalogues, programmes; signage.

Some graphic designers prefer to delegate and are known as artistic directors. They organize the work of others, ensuring that the group's production is of a satisfactory standard. Others work alone and do not delegate. Which approach is taken is purely a matter of personality; the end result is the same.

The principal qualities which make a good graphic designer are creativity, sensitivity and a thoughtful approach. Certain graphic artists suffer from inhibition or from an excessive desire to please. Outstanding projects are often based around a sudden change in direction where the designer adopts a type style which is universally despised and attempts to turn it into something interesting. The pitfall for some graphic designers is to repeat what they do best, creating a series of similar designs and ending up with a set of graphic clichés. Worse still, some designers fail to develop their project beyond the first rough sketch. It is in fact always difficult to move on from the sketch to the full-scale design; any inadequacy in the design which does not appear in the reduced-scale drawing becomes all too apparent in the full-scale model. Here the professional talent for 'fine tuning' comes into play. The overall concept, in its broadest sense, can take in a number of different elements, or ideas: the combination of certain colours, the choice of a word, the creation of three-dimensional effect, or whatever. But behind every piece of work there must be an idea. The graphic artist invites the observer's attention by means of visual witticisms, puzzles, ambiguous images, provocativeness and style. His or her skill lies in achieving a subtle balance between provocativeness and communication, between legibility and form.

A professional graphic artist designs and produces images which fulfil certain criteria:

The idea must be original and the design must make an impact.

The graphic form must be appropriate to its underlying meaning.

There must be clarity of intention.

There must be a maximum of expression to convey the necessary information.

The structure and layout must be suitable for their function.

The graphics must be legible so that their message can be readily recognized.

All visual languages and those creations which use them must fulfil these criteria. Only then can one ensure that the signifier is appropriate to the signified, whatever vocabulary is used.

Concept, object and method

The concept of visual identity has evolved over the last fifty years, and nowadays the majority of large bodies, whether they be public or private, have their own visual identity strategy. Visual identity is generally defined as a means of communicating in a memorable way the characteristics which are central to an organization. It is fair to say that every institution, whatever its size, has a visual identity which is either official or unofficial and which may or may not be in keeping with an overall communications strategy. Such a strategy is not a universal cure for problems of communication, nor must it be regarded as a cosmetic means for representing the organization as something which it is not. In order to create a visual identity, it is necessary to study the history of the institution, its current situation and its future direction. Such a project is part of long-term planning and is an integral part of the overall strategy of the organization. The creation of a visual identity is the most complex of all processes of graphic design, and it is therefore essential to obtain the support of the client's executive directors, as much for the creation of the identity as for its maintenance.

Visual identity projects can in general be grouped into three categories:

the modification of an already existing identity

the creation of an identity for a new organization

the creation of an identity for an already well-known organization.

The same fundamental idea, however, underlies them all. Everything that the institution does, everything that belongs to it and every service that it offers must project a clear image of that body and of its objectives. Whether it is an identity for an organization or for a temporary exhibition, the method remains the same and takes place in four stages:

1 *Analysis of the client*
2 *Establishment of a design brief and graphic strategy*
3 *Development of the graphic identity*
4 *Applications of the graphics*

These four stages take place over a fairly lengthy period, during which dialogue between the graphic artist and the client will make possible the definition and attainment of a common goal.

1 *Analysis*

This stage allows for the problem to be defined, objectives to be decided upon, for a review of the identity which already exists and for an audience and targets to be identified. This analysis, or audit, is carried out by means of meetings with directors, curators, public relations officers, visitor liaison staff and the print department, all of whom must set out their objectives. Questionnaires, interviews and site visits complement this series of meetings, providing the designer with both an internal and external view of the institution. At the same time, an inventory of existing printed material, such as stationery and leaflets, must be compiled.

2 *Design brief and graphic strategy*

Following this analytical stage, the drawing up of a design brief, or programme, allows the graphic artist to begin to look for some kind of strategy. The brief puts forward the objectives the project must meet; these are identified by assessing the evidence accumulated during the detailed analysis of the client. The brief varies according to the complexity of the institution or event, but it will always be the key to the later stage of formulating the identity's rules. In effect, the brief defines the project. It must indicate that the nature of the project has been fully understood – its scope, its aims and its limits. It must provide the client with a document which can be used during all stages of the design process and which can be used as a guide when comparing the proposed designs. The following concerns must be dealt with: the nature of the subject; programme objectives; strategy in terms of communications and brand image; users; official languages; budget; production; marketing; distribution and sales.

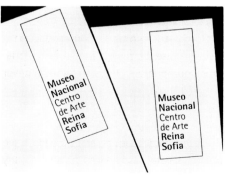

Two recent examples of logos from the Spanish-speaking world: the Museo de Arte Moderno in Mexico City (designed by Magda Gonzalez) and the Centro de Arte Reina Sofia, Madrid.

Massimo Vignelli's poster, catalogue and announcement for the European Iceberg Exhibition (Toronto, 1984).

The more information about a client's past, its competitors and structure is made available to a graphic artist, over and above the main lines of its communications strategy, the more effective will be his or her response. The graphic artist must also take into account the technical implications of specific uses of the identity, so that the overall concept does not have to be modified later for technical reasons.

A graphic strategy is worked out by producing a series of rough sketches and by experimenting with logotypes, colours and alphabets. By considering the application of the design for use on letterheads, sign system or publications, the graphic artist can formalize the overall concept and verify that the sketches fulfil the requirements. The logo, if there is one, must take into account certain considerations, such as whether it is possible to reduce its size and whether there are possibilities for adjustment.

3   Development of the graphic identity

After reaching agreement with the commissioning institution on the graphic strategies to be used, the graphic artist refines the sketches and visualizes the broad outlines for the application and development of his or her design, taking into account any requirements for the reproduction of the image. At this stage, an evaluation of the client's reproduction facilities, both internal and external, is of great importance. Only after these have been assessed can the graphic artist guarantee the fullest exploitation of the visual image and present a viable graphic project to the client. Every identity system depends on a series of complex rules which stipulate with precision the way in which the image can be used. This phase in the project is therefore particularly crucial.

4   Applications

Having secured the approval of the client, the graphic artist produces and prints the first images and in addition puts forward a design standards manual. This sets out a whole series of models showing how the identity should be applied in all foreseeable situations. The guidelines are a crucial reference book which must be consulted and followed if the image is to be effective. The manual is aimed at the various specialists involved in the project (curators, public relations officers, designers, typesetters and printers) and becomes a practical tool in the whole process of design and production. Ideally, graphic rules should establish a framework or structure without imposing limits on the process of creation. Given that visual communications and design are dynamic activities, it is necessary to establish a balance between strict rules and those guidelines which allow for a certain degree of flexibility and which encourage innovation.

The list of applications of the image, which will all be guided by the models in the design standards manual, varies according to the breadth of the institution's communications strategy: it can include a symbol, stationery, publications, a sign system, transport, packaging and other related products or services.

The estimation of the cost of the project can be worked out in stages as it takes shape, either through a series of meetings or in the early stages of development. As an example of the costs which might be incurred, in 1983 the Musée d'Orsay spent 2.3 million francs on a project which included its institutional identity and sign system. Production costs were 5 million francs.

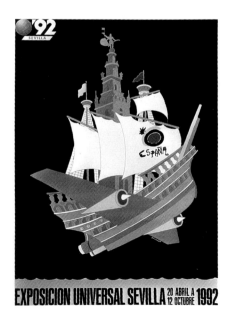

The Pushpin Group's poster for the universal exposition in Seville, 1992 (illustration and design by Seymour Chwast/The Pushpin Group).

The future of museums

The museum has become a centre for communication, a rallying point and a place of cultural union. But amid the current burgeoning of artistic activities, there lurk a number of dangerous side-effects which have to be avoided.

First of all, museums must not make the mistake of treating everything as though it were in a showcase, to 'mummify' everything. It is also undesirable to cause the stagnation of the art market; this had its hour of glory when the rash of new museums boosted demand, but it cannot continue creating supply and demand on its own. It would be perilous to emphasize the profitability of a museum to the detriment of genuine artistic and cultural criteria, whether elitist or popular. Institutions must, moreover, ensure that they do not accumulate important collections without the means to conserve them or to make them part of a living museum.

Art institutions must take care that they do not succumb to any of these pitfalls. The way to do this is to develop a strategy for the future built upon a concerted determination to put on programmes of special events; to take a sympathetic approach to the needs of visitors; and to adopt a more rigorous management of their identity systems. At the same time, they must not become too uniform as a group; they must leave room for a multiplicity of styles to develop and flourish.

The language of graphic design: glossary of terms

Alphabet: a type style which is used consistently.

Colour code: choice of colours and rules as to their use.

Compatible typography: a type style that complements the *signature* and is used for supplementary copy, such as address blocks and advertisements.

Corporate colours: the colour combination chosen to represent the company, to be used wherever possible.

Corporate identity: a designed image acquired and communicated by the company to the public through consistent visual communications.

Grid: outline of the layout structure, setting out margins and the locations of texts and images.

Identity system: a system of visual communications, graphically coordinated in such a way that the public easily identifies the company and its activities.

Logotype: the company name, designed in a unique and individual form. This does not include setting the name in an existing type style. Logotypes are always made up of letters, either a full name or initials.

Mark: a visual device designed specifically to identify graphically a particular organization or product in a way that is unique, appropriate and relevant. Different organizations will use different terms to describe their mark: for instance, it will be a symbol, trademark or logotype to a company, while a club will speak of its 'badge', or a publishing house of its 'colophon'. It may also be referred to as an emblem, insignia or branding. Designers usually divide marks into three categories: *symbols*, *logotypes* and *monograms*.

Master artwork: a film negative or positive of approved *signature* arrangements (flush left, centred, flush right, negative, and so on). Master artwork alone should be used for reproduction.

Monogram: a *mark* made up of intertwined or connected letters.

Signature: the company name (*logotype*) and *symbol* used as a unit in a variety of arrangements that describe the company, its divisions, or its activities.

Symbol: an abstract or pictorial graphic device (*mark*) that distinguishes a company, its activities and its product and promotes immediate identification of these by the public.

AMERICA

This museum, founded in 1979 and known as 'MOCA', houses works of art created since the early 1940s. It was brought into being as the result of an alliance between private initiative and the mayor's office. Land was offered by the city's Community Redevelopment Agency. It now occupies two buildings, the main one of which was designed by the Japanese architect Arata Isozaki and was opened in 1986. The other, called the Temporary Contemporary, is a former warehouse renovated by Frank Gehry in 1983.

Through its temporary exhibitions and its permanent collection, MOCA has become an international centre reflecting contemporary art in all its forms – video, film, sculpture and so on. The museum is involved in commissioning and displaying new art installations at the Temporary Contemporary, while in the main building permanent and temporary exhibitions are staged in a more conventionally reverent manner. Other museum activities include dance performances, multimedia displays, a publishing programme and the purchase of works of art.

The museum's graphics programme has several aspects and it employs different designers to fulfil different functions. It has actively taken the decision to avoid a monolithic visual image, apart from on its administrative stationery.

The stationery revolves around three simple geometric forms – the square, the circle and the triangle – in association with the primary colours yellow, blue,

Museum of Contemporary Art
Los Angeles

Designers Chermayeff & Geismar Associates: Ivan Chermayeff, Keith Helmetag. Cross Associates. Pentagram: Kit Hinrichs. Lorraine Wild. *Work done* Logotype, stationery, sign system, exhibition graphics, brochures *Year* 1985–89

and red, as well as green. This logo is repeated on other items intended to be seen by the public and designed by other graphic artists: for instance, on the front of the family guide (Pentagram).

The free-hand 'T' enigmatically emphasizes the 'T's in the 'Temporary Contemporary' and provides a contrast to the severity of the geometric forms. The stationery is in line with a graphics trend of the 1980s, which restored value to simple, basic shapes allied with free-hand typography.

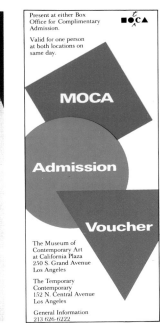

Present at either Box
Office for Complimentary
Admission.

Valid for one person
at both locations on
same day.

MOCA

Admission

Voucher

The Museum of
Contemporary Art
at California Plaza
250 S. Grand Avenue
Los Angeles

The Temporary
Contemporary
152 N. Central Avenue
Los Angeles

General Information
213 626-6222

Members
Calendar

11.19–2.18

Issue 4, 1989

Sylvia Hohri
Marketing and
Graphics Manager

250 South Grand Avenue
at California Plaza
Los Angeles, California 90012
(213) 621-2766
Telex: MOCA 194476

MUSEUM OF CONTEMPORARY ART, LOS ANGELES

Page 17: the museum's logo contrasts basic geometric shapes with a hand-written 'T' representing the Temporary Contemporary. Its flexibility makes it ideally suited for use in a wide variety of situations (*opposite page*) including stationery (Chermayeff & Geismar); the Members Calendar (Cross Associates); free admission vouchers; and (*this page*) a family guide (Pentagram).

The family guide is immediately attractive to children because of the brilliance of its colour and the unusual pattern produced by cutting the edges of its pages into geometric shapes. The grid on which it is constructed is broken up by a multitude of free-style drawings. The guide is available in each of the five major languages spoken in Los Angeles.

WELCOME TO MOCA! THIS GUIDE IS WRITTEN TO INTRODUCE YOU AND YOUR FAMILY TO CONTEMPORARY ART. IT CONTAINS IDEAS TO HELP YOU LOOK AT AND THINK AND TALK ABOUT THE CONTEMPORARY ART IN THE GALLERIES. THE EXAMPLES OF THE ART WORKS IN THIS GUIDE ARE SOME OF OUR FAVORITES AT MOCA. THE GUIDE IS ONLY A SUGGESTION; THE REST IS UP TO YOU! WE WANT YOU TO ENJOY THE ART, AT YOUR OWN PACE AND WITH YOUR FAMILY.

PARENTS: DURING YOUR VISIT

1. **Ask** your child to **lead** you to works of art. What is she/he looking at? Enjoying?

2. **Talk!** Museums are social places, so talk to each other. No need to whisper! Speak with the other families in the museum. Chances are, they will be curious to know your thoughts about the works of art.

3. **Share** your thoughts with your child. "I love the feeling of this sculpture... the way it glows. How do you suppose the artist made it glow?"

4. **Imagine** with your child. "What if the portrait was of someone who lived next door? What would it look like? What materials could we use?"

5. **Move** around the galleries or rooms within the museum. Look at an art work up close and from across the room. Compare an art work with the others in the exhibition. What do you notice?

6. Be **comfortable** in the galleries. **Sit** on the floor or borrow a stool from the Information Center.

7. Help your child **think**. Connect the experience to something in your child's life. "Remember how the sky looked and the air felt during the rainstorm last week?"

8. **Praise** your child. Use phrases such as "Your answer helped me see something in this painting..."

9. Your **mood** will affect your child, so focus on the visit and your child.

10. **Some days** are better than others. If things don't work out, try the museum's **other building**. Or, try it another day.

11. **Read** the information about each work of art in this Family Guide. Read it aloud or ask your child to read it aloud. Look at the art work again. How does the information affect your views of the art work now?

12. When discussing works of **art**, refer to the artist by name and the art work by its title.

13. **Read more.** There is information in the Gallery Guide and in *The Contemporary*. The bookstore has books, catalogs, magazines, videos and slides. Browse!

14. **Questions?** Ask anyone at the Information Center or ask a guard.

15. Take a **break**. Your ticket enables you to come in and out of both MOCA buildings all day long.

16. Don't feel that you have to see the **entire** museum or even the entire exhibition. Take your time.

17. Contemporary art elicits a variety of **reactions**. Ask your child **why** she/he is responding the way she/he is. What did the **artist** do to inspire the feelings?

18. The **goal** is to involve yourselves in art and respond to what you see. There are no **right** or **wrong** answers. The quest is the exploration of your own ideas about art. **Knowledge** and **awareness** will grow with future visits and by reading.

19. Please **don't touch** works of art. The moisture in your hands damages the works of art, that damage is often only visible under a microscope, but in time the art work will deteriorate.

20. Have **fun!** Get to know MOCA and its collections with your family and at your own pace.

CHILDREN:

1. **Choose** works of art that interest you.

2. **Talk** to your parents about what you see.

3. **Help** your parents really look at works of art. You'll see things that your parents won't.

4. **Tell** your parents if you are tired or hungry.

5. **Please don't touch** the works of art. The moisture in your hands damages the works of art.

6. This guide will help you use your **imagination** when looking at art!

HERE'S WHAT YOU CAN DO

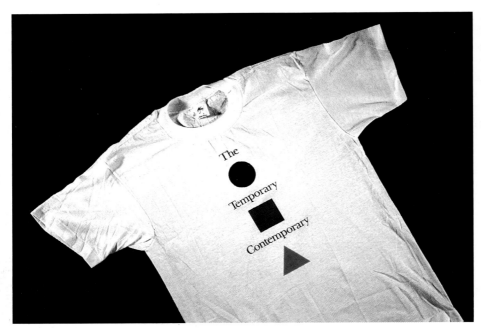

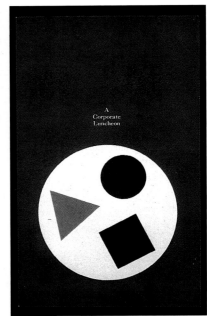

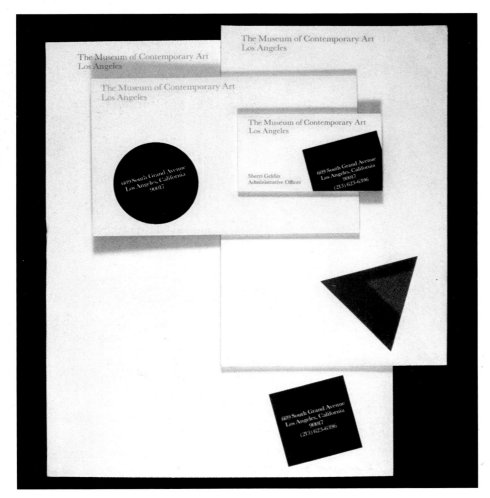

The commissions for the various facets of MOCA's identity programme were spread among the graphic designers as follows:

Chermayeff & Geismar Associates: logotype, promotional literature and posters, including one for the 1984 exhibition entitled 'Automobile and Culture', for the Temporary Contemporary. Logotype, fund-raising literature, sign system and promotional items for Isozaki's building. Stationery.

Cross Associates: pocket folder, *The Contemporary* (newspaper), Members Calendar.

Pentagram: family guide.

Lorraine Wild: gallery guides.

Despite all the variety in the museum's use of graphics, every item is of a high standard, reflecting the museum's commitment to the first-rate display of contemporary art.

MUSEUM OF CONTEMPORARY ART, LOS ANGELES

Opposite : T-shirt, stationery, a lunch and dinner invitation, all carrying early variants on the museum's logo.

This page : two posters by Chermayeff & Geismar for the Temporary Contemporary. One announces its opening in 1983 (*left*), the other (*above*) a temporary exhibition held in 1984.

New York International Festival of the Arts
New York

Designer Chermayeff & Geismar Associates: Ivan Chermayeff, William Anton (art director)
Work done Visual identity for promotional material
Year 1988

The New York International Festival of the Arts is a non-profit organization run by a board of directors who are outstanding leaders in the arts, business and international affairs. It was first held in summer 1988, when its supporters were able to choose from more than 350 events – music and opera, dance, theatre and film from the twentieth century – from over 20 nations.

Chermayeff & Geismar's brief was to create a distinct identification programme that would promote the festival. They were asked to design the tools that others could then use to implement the graphics for individual institutions, programmes and performances.

What the designers came up with was a unique alphabet with special characters for major categories of the festival: dance, film, music and opera, theatre. Design applications included posters, promotional publications and materials, invitations, programmes, banners, badges and T-shirts. The identity was based on the systematic use of word images, each one reflecting some aspect of the festival events or a place in New York. For instance:

E   piano keyboard
I   Doric column; or the Empire State Building
O   a tragic and comic mask; or a cello
Y   Statue of Liberty
'THE'   a strip of film

The resulting alphabet was then used on all information leaflets for the headings. The alphabet could be printed in several ways: in strong, basic colours against black or white; reversed out against a coloured background; or a single colour on white. A classic typography was used for the texts, which were set in a single column to the right of the headings.

The alphabet is very easy to read, an effect assisted by interspersing the 'word-image' letters with 'normal' ones. It successfully creates the atmosphere of a sizable arts festival where the applied and decorative arts coexist in cheerful harmony.

The designers' unique alphabet in action on a poster and information leaflets.

The Walker Art Center, which grew from the private collection of T.B. Walker, was opened in 1879. Since the 1940s, it has developed its design activities, both product and graphic. The permanent collection includes 20th-century works in the field of the plastic arts, such as photography, design and architecture. Temporary exhibitions are often complemented by live events. The terraces provide a series of bases for sculptures to attract visitors. Large exhibition banners, visible from the nearby highway, advertise temporary shows. The Center publishes catalogues and brochures, as well as the journal *Design Quarterly*.

The Center's visual identity, developed by Lorraine Ferguson, operates through the lettering on the museum's signs (including banners) and through poster visuals. A standard typeface is used for all contexts, following an excellent hierarchical system which enables information on the Center's permanent and temporary exhibitions to be easily read. The signs harmonize with the size of the building and have a strongly contemporary feel. The exterior signs, which let the public know what is currently on show, appear quite varied because of the non-uniform treatment of their texts – for instance the use of different colours, different weights or sizes for the letters, upper and lower case. They are, however, unified by their consistent typeface. The banner suspended against the building's façade to advertise the permanent collection is arranged like an enlarged book-cover and evokes the image of a picture hanging from a rail. On

Walker Art Center
Minneapolis

Designers **Lorraine Ferguson. Studio Dumbar (1982 poster)**
Work done **Sign system, posters, publications**
Year **1982 (poster); 1985–88**

the temporary exhibitions banners, events are readily identifiable, thanks to white lettering reversed out against broad coloured bands.

The advertisement on the restaurant wall for the temporary exhibition 'Sculpture Inside Outside' is typographic. The background against which the letters are set is coopted into playing an active part in the graphics game: the letters 'Outside' are formed from photographs of the sky, which produces the illusion of windows to the world outdoors. The names of the sculptors represented in the exhibition add the finishing touches to this artistically arranged composition; the names, each taking up two rows, are set in a line beneath the title and then rise up in two columns on either side of it.

WALKER ART CENTER

The Center's visual identity is typographic. A standard typeface provides unity, while different letter sizes and colours create variety. *Previous page and this page, left*: exterior exhibition banners (approx. 25 × 40 feet, 7½ × 12 metres). *Below*: exhibition graphics in the restaurant for a temporary show in 1988.

Opposite, left and below right: examples of printed material designed in-house. The Center commissions outside designers for specific projects: for instance, a poster (*above right*) by Studio Dumbar, the Netherlands, for the De Stijl exhibition (1982).

Please join us
for a Members' Opening of two major exhibitions

Jan Dibbets

Elizabeth Murray
Paintings and Drawings

Walker Art Center   Hors d'oeuvres
9 pm to midnight   Cash bar
Saturday   Keyboard compositions
30 January 1988   by Thomas Hiel
$7.50 per person   10:30 pm to midnight

Jan Dibbets
Minneapolis 1986–87
Hennepin County Government Center
color photographs,
watercolor, pencil and glass-pencil
on paper mounted on chipboard
74½ x 74½ inches
Private collection

Jan Dibbets

This exhibition
continues through
27 March 1988.

A major figure in European contemporary art, Jan Dibbets
has created a memorable body of work, much of it rooted
in the illustrious tradition of twentieth-century Dutch
abstraction. His photo-constructions, which incorporate
drawing and painting, show the shaping effects of the
conceptual and minimalist tendencies of the late 1960s.
Recent works, especially his lyrical interiors of cathedrals
and other monumental buildings, have become increasingly
expressive, moving toward an imagery that is more
romantic than analytical. This is the first major American
museum survey of the work of this internationally
recognized Dutch artist.

Jan Dibbets was organized by Walker Art Center in association with
the Stedelijk Van Abbemuseum, Eindhoven, The Netherlands. Support
for the exhibition has been provided by the National Endowment for
the Arts, KLM Royal Dutch Airlines and the Dutch Ministry of Welfare,
Public Health and Cultural Affairs.

Elizabeth Murray
Sail Baby 1983
oil on canvas
126 x 135 inches
Collection Walker Art Center
Walker Special Purchase Fund

Elizabeth Murray
Paintings and Drawings

The artist will be
present at the opening.

This exhibition
continues through
27 March 1988.

Elizabeth Murray's energetic, color-filled canvases have
established her as a major figure in recent American art. So
arresting are the components of Murray's imagery that they
seem to explode into three-dimensional forms. This
presentation of Murray's paintings and drawings illuminates
the evolution of her unique imagery, beginning with the
sinuous biomorphic forms she employed in the mid-1970s
to the dramatic variations on such everyday objects as cups
and saucers, tables, artists' palettes and abstracted parts of
human figures that characterize her work today.

Elizabeth Murray: Paintings and Drawings has been organized by the
Dallas Museum of Art and the Committee on the Visual Arts,
Massachusetts Institute of Technology, with the aid of generous grants
from the National Endowment for the Arts and the Massachusetts
Council on the Arts and Humanities.

VISIONS OF UTOPIA

DE STIJL 1917–1931

WALKER ART CENTER, MINNEAPOLIS, 31 JANUARY – 28 MARCH 1982
HIRSHHORN MUSEUM AND SCULPTURE GARDEN, WASHINGTON D.C.
18 APRIL – 27 JUNE 1982
STEDELIJK MUSEUM, AMSTERDAM, 8 AUGUST – 25 SEPTEMBER 1982
KRÖLLER-MÜLLER, OTTERLO, 8 AUGUST – 3 OCTOBER 1982

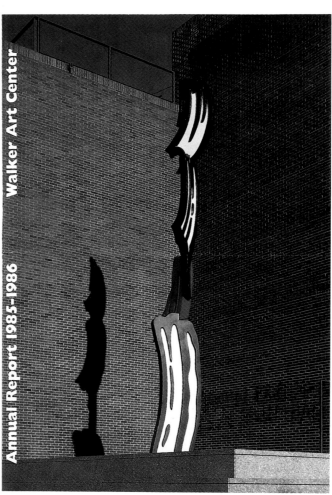

Walker Art Center

Annual Report 1985–1986

Tokyo Arts Festival

April-July 1986

A four month festival of Film, Performing Arts, and Education events offered in conjunction with *Tokyo: Form and Spirit*

Presenting a dynamic view of the arts in Japan today, Tokyo Arts Festival reflects the continuity of tradition in even the most contemporary of artistic expressions. These events reveal the foundations of Japan's classical, folk and avant-garde cultural life.

Tokyo: Form and Spirit is an extensive exhibition, which draws parallels between four centuries of Japanese art, architecture and design.

Including both important examples of Japanese design from Tokyo's Edo Period (1603-1868) and visionary contemporary spaces commissioned from leading Japanese architects and designers, *Tokyo: Form and Spirit* offers a glimpse into the heart of Japan, such as is rarely offered to

outsiders even today. From the traditional to the most vanguard, the exhibition presents new insights into Japanese attitudes toward the individual, the family, the city, commerce and society, illustrating the longevity of underlying themes of Japanese life.

Tokyo: Form and Spirit is organized around activities of daily life in the Japanese capital city, Tokyo. *Walking* is symbolized by a section devoted to the

street; *Living*, by the house; *Working*, by the shop and factory; *Performing*, by the theater; *Reflecting*, by the temple; and *Playing*, by the playground. Each thematic area contains both an Edo and a contemporary section.

Admission price to *Tokyo: Form and Spirit* is $3.50; $2, senior citizens. Members of the Walker are admitted free at all times. The exhibition is free to the public all Thursdays. Hours are 10 am-8 pm,

Tues.-Sat.; 11 am-5 pm Sundays. The museum is closed Mondays.

Major funding for *Tokyo: Form and Spirit* has come from: National Endowment for the Humanities; First Bank Minneapolis; "Close-Up of Japan" by the Mitsui Group; Honeywell Inc.; SONY Co., Ltd.; Japan-United States Friendship Commission; The Japan Foundation; and The Hitachi Foundation.

Walker Art Center

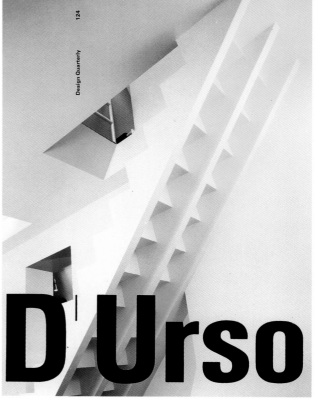

WALKER ART CENTER

Opposite : poster for the Tokyo Arts Festival, celebrated at the Center in 1986. *This page* : a selection of covers for *Design Quarterly*, together with a poster-cum-subscription form.

AIGA: The American Institute of Graphic Arts
New York

Designers **Various**
Work done **Posters, leaflets**
Year **1986–89**

The American Institute of Graphic Arts is a national non-profit organization, founded in 1914, with more than twenty chapters in cities across the States. It runs a programme of competitions, exhibitions, publications and educational activities to promote excellence in graphic design. AIGA's members work in every area of the graphic arts: corporate, environmental and promotional graphics, publishing, illustration, advertising and exhibitions. The institute reaches a wider audience by sponsoring projects in the public interest.

At intervals, AIGA launches competitions open to both members and non-members on payment of an entrance fee. Themes and categories are carefully defined, and only items produced in the USA or Canada during a specified period are eligible. Accepted works are all hung in an exhibition and appear in the institute's annual, *Graphic Design USA*. The competition is announced through posters and leaflets of varying formats. On the back of the poster, the rules, the names of the jurors (who change each year) and category definitions are set forth. The layout and first-rate typography selected for this 'Call for Entries' are often more creative than the visual image on the front of the poster.

A selection of 'Call for Entries' posters gives an idea of their scope.

1986 'AIGA Book Show': a competition to find the most outstanding books originated and designed in the USA and Canada during 1986. Dugald Stermer's design adapts the dolphin and anchor symbol of the famous Aldine Press in Venice. Pastel shades of green, brown and purple stand out against a salmon background. The handwritten nature of the text is emphasized by leaving the pencil guidelines visible.

1986 'One Color Two Color': the intention of the show was to encourage the use of strong, elegant images using only a few colours, in contrast to the trend of using a multitude. People needed to be reminded that less can mean more. The poster, by Michael Mabry Design, echoes a 1920s style from Germany. The colours used are red and black on bistre-tinted paper.

1987 'Design for the Public Good': the exhibition was open to graphic work of all kinds which communicated international public concerns, such as

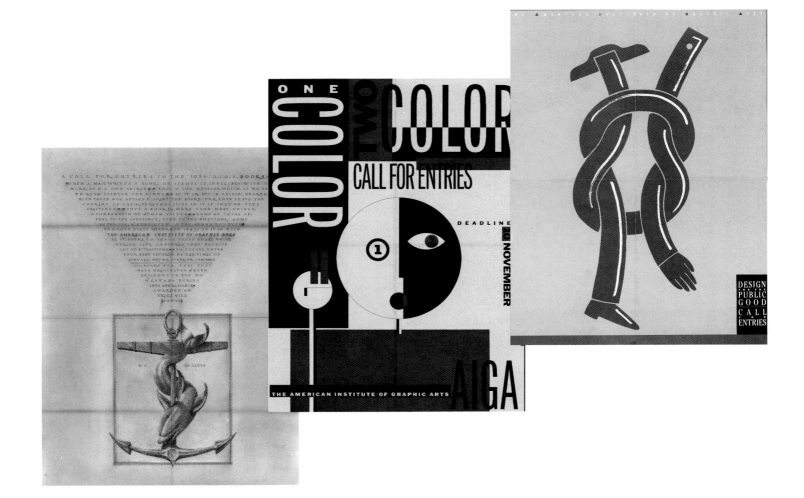

peace, saving energy, funding or promoting the arts. The poster, designed by Lanny Sommese and Kristin Breslin, consists of a monochrome illustration representing tools (hammers and ruler), interlinked with a human arm and leg.

1989 'People, Places & Things': all forms of graphic communication which were printed between 1984 and 1989 and which involved illustration or photography related to the exhibition theme were eligible. The poster was designed by Fred Woodward and Gail Anderson, and included a photograph of a classical bust and the competition title in gold lettering.

1989 'Communication Graphics': work printed in 1988 was eligible. The poster, designed by Sametz Blackstone Associates, features 'AIGA' in computer graphics. On the back is an interesting typographic composition in which two different texts are printed on alternate lines, one in red, the other in black.

1989 'Insides Outsides': the competition examined both the insides and outsides of a wide range of categories for printed matter: covers of magazines, record sleeves, page layouts, graphs and charts. Richard Turtletaub's poster takes various images and playfully manipulates them to reflect the competition title in a surrealist style.

A selection of 'Call for Entries' posters for AIGA's design competitions.

Opposite, left to right: 'AIGA Book Show' (1986, Dugald Stermer): the symbol of the Aldine Press represents the well-designed book. 'One Color Two Color' (1986, Michael Mabry Design): the restricted palette of red and black demonstrates the show's theme. 'Design for the Public Good' (1987, Lanny Sommese and Kristin Breslin): tools are inextricably intertwined with a human being, who uses them to benefit the human race.

Left: the reverse of the 'Communication Graphics' poster (1989, Sametz Blackstone Associates) features two interlocking texts, printed on alternate lines. They are differentiated by the use of red and black and by the difference in size of their letters. *Above*: 'Insides Outsides' offers a montage of disparate images (1989, Richard Turtletaub), while 'People, Places & Things' is represented by a photograph of a classical bust (1989, Fred Woodward and Gail Anderson).

International Design Conference in Aspen

Aspen

Designers Pentagram: Alan Fletcher (1986), Woody Pirtle (1988). Italo Lupi (1989)
Work done Visual symbol, information and promotional material
Year 1986, 1988, 1989

The international conferences in Aspen, Colorado, on design (both product, architectural and graphic) have taken place every year since 1950. They enjoy a world-wide reputation, and are open only to professionals. Each year a different theme is chosen, around which debates, conferences and films are organized. The commission for the event's graphics is awarded annually to a different designer.

The theme of the 36th conference (1986) was 'Insight and Outlook: Views of British Design'. Kenneth Grange, a partner in Pentagram, was co-chairman that year, and Pentagram's Alan Fletcher (London office) designed the symbol for the conference. He employed one of the world's greatest visual clichés, a flag – and, moreover, the Union Jack. It appeared on posters, invitations, T-shirts, badges and other promotional material. The graphics brought together free-hand treatment and geometric austerity, while still abiding by the pattern of the flag.

The 38th conference (1988) focused on the current state of design in the global community. To define graphically 'The Cutting Edge' theme, Woody Pirtle (Pentagram, New York) designed a graphic system featuring a harlequin balancing on the edge of a razor as its central image, to illustrate the precariousness of producing adventurous work. The programme included brochures, folders, posters, mailing cards and an events guide.

The visuals for the 1989 conference book cover, designed by Italo Lupi, were based on the theme title 'The Italian Manifesto'. The graphics make a game out of reading the title: various geometric shapes form the bare outline of the letters, imaginary elements of the typography cut out from coloured paper.

The above selection is representative of the attention paid by the conference organizers to graphics, and also of the highly professional standard of those designers who are commissioned, which forms a symbiosis with the standard of those attending the event.

Left: Alan Fletcher chose the Union Jack as the symbol for the 1986 conference, which had British design as its theme. The image combines the geometric precision of the red cross with the hand-crayoned effect of the blue diagonals.

Opposite, above: Woody Pirtle emphasized the difficulties of creating adventurous work by his memorable image for the 1988 conference, which explored the theme of 'The Cutting Edge'. A silhouette harlequin balances on the edge of a gleaming razor, while the jagged black and yellow pattern suggests sharpness and danger.

Opposite, below: Italo Lupi's design for the programme book cover (1989). The title, *The Italian Manifesto*, is made up of a variety of geometric cut-outs which merely hint at the letter shapes, thus inviting the readers to solve the puzzle for themselves.

Insight and Outlook. Views of British Design. **36th International Design Conference in Aspen. Sunday, June 15 to Friday, June 20, 1986.** Aspen '86 explores the diversity and vitality of British design today. **Conference Co-chairmen Kenneth Grange,** Pentagram London, and **Rosamind Julius,** Julius International, are asking – Why Britain? Is British design strong despite or because of a hostile cultural environment? Why do young designers go it alone? Historical heritage – millstone or milestone? Do national characteristics of eccentricity, irony and understatement affect design in today's international business world. Topics range from fashion, photography, film, graphics, advertising, architecture, interiors and product design to theatre and gardens. Speakers include architects **Norman Foster** and **James Stirling;** photographer **Norman Parkinson;** artist **David Hockney;** film producer **David Puttnam;** fashion designer **Bruce Oldfield;** graphic designer **Alan Fletcher;** cartoonist **Ralph Steadman;** Head of Royal College of Art **Jocelyn Stevens;** Director of The Victoria and Albert Museum **Sir Roy Strong.** Work of emerging young designers will be shown in presentations, workshops and exhibitions. General Foods will sponsor International Fellows. **Special events:** fashion show, workshops, a week of British films, "Spitting Image" comedy event, picnics and British foods, cricket match. Steering Committee: Niels Diffrient, Milton Glaser, Frank Stanton. **Regular registration:** $425 (US dollars). **Early bird registration:** $375 (if received by May 1). One additional member of household: $200. Full time student: $125. (photocopy of current ID required with registration). List all applicants by name. Make check payable to IDCA and mail to: IDCA c/o Bank of Aspen, PO Box O, Aspen, CO 81612. **Further information:** IDCA, PO Box 664, Aspen, CO 81612, (303) 925-2257.

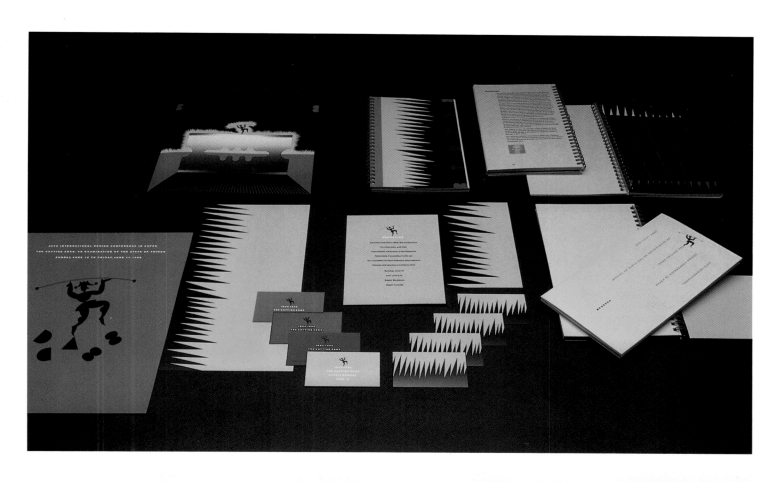

39TH INTERNATIONAL DESIGN CONFERENCE IN ASPEN, 13-18 JUNE 1989

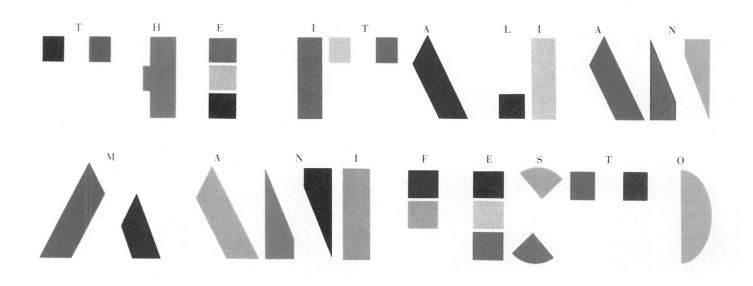

Katonah Museum of Art
Katonah

Designer Chermayeff & Geismar Associates
Work done Logo and folder design (Stephan Geissbuhler, partner); brochure design (Cathy Rediehs), 1986. Logo redesign (Stephen Loges); design of typeface and applications (Anthony McKenzie Williams), 1989
Year 1986, 1989

The Katonah Museum of Art provides cultural and educational enrichment for the people of New York and Connecticut. It has no permanent collection, but displays selections of the best of art from the past to the present, as well as providing art education and exhibiting the works of artists from the surrounding area.

The museum was formerly known as 'The Katonah Gallery', but changed its name to 'Katonah Museum of Art' to emphasize its status as a museum rather than a gallery. The change of name required a redesign of identity, and both were managed to coincide with the opening of a new museum building in October 1990 (by architects Edward Larrabee Barnes).

The new logo, a skilful adaptation of the previous one, was, like its predecessor, designed by Chermayeff & Geismar Associates. It is applied to stationery, signage, promotional and exhibit-related materials.

The identity calls upon simple rules and a functional aesthetic which has connections with the Swiss school of the 1970s. It consists of a 'K', formed by putting together three outward-facing triangles (green and blue) and a square (red) balanced in the space to the right. Taken together, the geometric shapes form a larger square.

The colours of the elements of the logo can be varied. For instance on the museum's stationery, it is printed in grey with one colour for the balancing square which produces the 'K': blue for news releases, red for letters from the directorate, and so on. Graphic coherence is established by the typography. The address and any other information are printed in the same pale grey.

There is no tyrannical graphic scheme, but instead numerous variations on the logo are created, in what could be seen as a passing reference to the principles of graphic design. The weight attached to detail gives added interest. With considerable exactingness and without any flashy extravagance, the identity imparts a real sense of freshness to very basic building blocks.

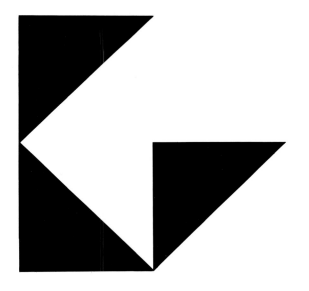

Left and below: the gallery's symbol, designed in 1986. 'KG' is cleverly created by putting together the minimum of geometric shapes – three black triangles.

Opposite: the identity was redesigned in 1989 to emphasize Katonah's status as a museum rather than a gallery. The three triangles are repositioned and a square is added. Instead of the triangles actually being the 'K', the 'K' is now the empty space fenced around by the geometric shapes.

 The Katonah Gallery

The basic colours of the symbol are blue, green and red. Various
changes can be rung upon it by printing the square in one of these
colours, the triangles in grey. The consistent, grey typography provides
coherence.

Katonah Museum of Art

International Design Center of New York

New York

Designer **Vignelli Associates: Massimo Vignelli, Michael Bierut**
Work done **Logo, journals, printed matter, bags, sign system**
Year **1983–89**

The Design Center (IDCNY) was opened in 1986 and is financed by industry and by wholesalers. Its objective is to display accomplished products and also certain designers' works that have been produced in limited editions. It is open both to the public and to professional members.

The building is in Long Island City, on the bank of the East River across from Manhattan. Four old factories from the late nineteenth century, with their massive interiors, have been converted into an exhibition area of a million square feet (about 93,000 square metres), with the potential to expand to 4 million square feet. The buildings' exteriors, especially an old chewing-gum and a battery factory, have been restored, but the interior has been utterly transformed by the New York architects Gwathmey Siegel. Two superb atria, around which the showrooms are built, are there to receive visitors. The entrance is impressive, nine storeys in height and more than 30 yards (about 28 metres) in length. The iron footbridges which connect the two parts of the composite building tone down its monumentalness.

Certain exhibitors have called upon architects with international reputations to design their showroom. Mario Botta, for example, designed the ICF showroom at the IDCNY, his first project in the United States.

The Center's logo picks up the initials IDCNY in upper case, using two different typefaces. The range of colours is red, black and white, red being dominant. The austere and masterly typography is sometimes underscored by narrow lines. The visuals make considerable use of photographs, either of products or tools. The images are freely positioned on the page, and the use of different scales adds vitality without losing the sobriety appropriate to the business world. Both the choice of visuals and the organization of the typography exactly suit industrial design and the world of everyday objects. The photography is used to introduce the real world, while the text is used to question or inform the public. The sign system makes use of giant letters, a reflection of the enormous size of the building, with an effective elegance.

Vignelli Associates' identity programme is based upon three very basic elements: the use of the Bodoni typeface and of the colours red and black. With these simple building blocks the designers have created a vibrant, well-articulated scheme which achieves a strong visual identity. *Opposite* : facade with exterior sign. *This page* : selection of printed material.

Children's Museum of Manhattan
New York

Designer Vignelli Associates: Michael Bierut, Alan Hopfensperger
Work Done Logo, stationery, information leaflets and promotional material
Year 1989

The museum was founded in 1973 and was opened to the public some time later, as part of the drive towards the development of museums for children. This movement drew inspiration in the 1960s from the work of the Swiss psychologist Jean Piaget, who showed the great importance for children of learning by questioning and examining their environment. The Manhattan museum presents both temporary and permanent exhibits and educational programmes for children of all ages; it also has an area devoted to the world of books. All the activities are based on education through creativity and on self-discovery, whether in the world of the arts, sciences or theatre. On each floor,

there are exhibits and activity centres where children can learn by doing, with the assistance of educators, artists-in-residence, scientific instructors and so on. The varied programme includes weekend and holiday performances of singers, dancers, puppeteers and storytellers; daily animation and television work-shops; and activities for pre-school-age girls and boys. Nearly 150,000 children and their families visit the museum each year.

The museum's identity consists of a logo made up from the initials CMOM. The symbol has great freshness, and achieves a successful equilibrium between free-hand expression and typographic rigour. The balance between the playful and the serious and the use of the typefaces Bodoni and Futura impart the sense of an original, personal style.

When the logo is adapted for use on information documents, great freedom is exercised. The use of colour (blue, yellow and red) for the subheadings, together with scattered letters from the logo, printed in different sizes and positions, gives a feeling of vitality. Added to these visuals, there is elegant typography and a distinctly 'architectural' look to the layout grid. In the period in which we live, in a society crammed full of things to be read, it is the style of the graphics that distinguishes one piece of literature from another. The Children's Museum's identity, with its expressiveness and straightforward colours, is bound to attract the attention of its potential public.

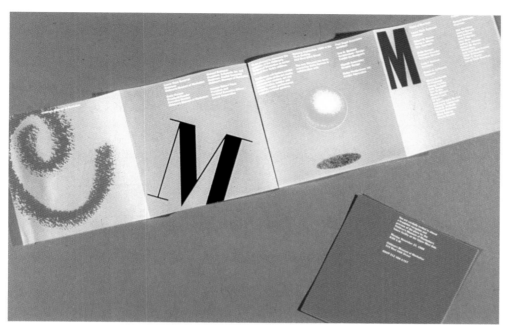

The aim of the designers was to create a playful, kinetic image suitable for Manhattan's only museum exclusively for children. This was achieved by rendering each of the initial letters CMOM in a different style and colour (basic logo, *above right*), then combining and recombining them in different sizes and scales on a wide range of materials.

Knot Exhibition
New York

Designer Vignelli Associates: Massimo Vignelli
Work done Poster, catalogue cover
Year 1985

The Knot was an exhibition organized by Germano Celant on the Italian Arte Povera movement and was held in 1985 at P.S.1, the Institute for Art and Urban Resources, Long Island City. The catalogue was fastened with a piece of real rope tied in a knot around a corrugated board, in order to express the movement's concern for strong, 'poor', natural materials. Produced by the Institute for Art and Urban Resources, Inc., New York, and Umberto Allemandi & Co., Turin, the catalogue is a combination of conceptual art and materials with which the designer felt great affinity. The poster, which featured a photograph of the knotted rope, was printed on kraft paper. When several were placed side by side, a continuous image was created. The poster was selected for inclusion in the permanent collection of Die Neue Sammlung in Munich.

Vignelli's design reflects the precision and elegance which are his trademark. From the 1960s, he has always applied the simple rules of legibility, of the concise and economical communication of information, and of achieving a good balance between the modern and classical. His creative work for the Knot clearly reveals his ability to compel recognition of his work, which steps outside the bounds of fashion. His visual theme and choice of presentational material are relevant to the subject, his typography and the ranging left and right of the various columns very contemporary in approach, while at the same time remaining classical.

Poster (*below left*) and catalogue (*below*) for the Knot exhibition on the Arte Povera movement. The catalogue is encircled by a length of real 'knotted' rope, which is transformed into a photograph on the poster. Vignelli's composition creates an impact by its precision and elegance.

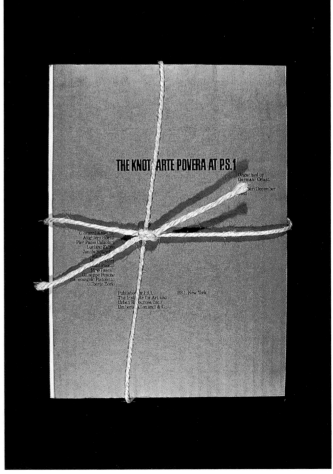

Brooklyn Museum
New York

Designer **Milton Glaser**
Work done **Poster**
Year **1985**

The Brooklyn Museum occupies a monumental building, complete with pediment and peristyle, a design typical of its architects McKim, Mead and White. Its five floors of exhibits contain rich and comprehensive collections which deserve to be better known. The main collections are: primitive arts (including masks, jewellery, pottery); items from the Middle and Far East (including paintings and ceramics); archaeological finds from Mediterranean, Near Eastern and Coptic antiquity (the Egyptian galleries are outstanding); furniture, decorative arts and costume; and finally painting and sculpture (including some modern works). The museum was the first to gather together an important and fascinating collection of architectural ornaments salvaged from demolished buildings for display in a sculpture garden.

It is the museum's originality in preserving the architectural heritage in the form of fragmentary blocks that provides the powerful source of inspiration for the illustrations on Glaser's poster. The title is actually superimposed on a drawing of a detached section of the museum building, surrounded by further elements notable for their exotic, decorative shapes.

Milton Glaser describes what he hoped to achieve with his poster as follows: 'The intention . . . was to encourage those living outside the borough of Brooklyn to come to the museum. The Brooklyn Museum itself is a building of distinguished architecture. The poster is made out of fragments of the total building shown below, enhanced with a variety of marbleized paper. The title, ''Visit a Masterpiece'', creates some ambiguity about whether the ''masterpiece'' is within the building or is the building itself. This is the sort of ambiguity we hope the viewer will find provocative and sufficiently interesting to generate a visit.'

The museum appears not to have a regular, permanent, graphics programme. Instead, it commissions well-known designers for various projects as the need arises.

Milton Glaser's poster attracts the viewer's attention by its ambiguity. Is it exhorting us to visit the museum to view the masterpieces it shelters within its walls? Or is the museum building itself the masterpiece we should visit?

The poster presents the viewer with dismembered fragments of the museum building in pastel shades – mainly pink, blue and grey, highlighted with red, orange and deep blue: a reference to the museum's innovative sculpture garden. The poster's text, 'Visit a Masterpiece', printed in black, is incorporated into the very fabric of the building by treating it as an inscription.

39

Museum of Modern Art
New York

Designers **Chermayeff & Geismar Associates: Ivan Chermayeff. Igarashi Studio. Steven Schoenfelder.**
Work done **Logos, stationery, bags, exhibition graphics, etc.**
Year **1984–91**

In 1929, just ten days after the stock market crash, the museum opened with an exhibition on Cézanne, Gauguin, Seurat and Van Gogh, then hardly known in the United States. Since then, the institution has pursued an original acquisitions policy, which embraced artistic fields such as photography, design and architecture before they achieved general recognition. The public has always shown an ever-increasing interest in the museum's activities and facilities, among them a library and cinema.

In 1939, the museum was able to move to its permanent home, designed by Philip Goodwin and Edward Durell Stone. This was extended considerably in the 1950s and '60s under the architect Philip Johnson, who also designed the Abby Aldrich Rockefeller Sculpture Garden. A major renovation, finished in 1984, doubled the museum's gallery space.

Famous for the quality and bold scope of the contemporary interests of its permanent collection, the museum is without equal in providing an overview of the modern movement. Its collection is sizable: by 1990, 10,000 works of art, including architectural models and design objects; 80,000 books and periodicals; 10,000 films and 3 million film stills.

The museum's policy on graphic communication is ad hoc; administrative stationery was designed by one studio, bags for its shop by another, periodicals by yet another. Most of the work is carried out by in-house designers within the museum itself, external designers being brought in apparently only for certain shows or events. The general impression created falls short of the high standard of the museum's reputation.

The museum's logo, designed by Ivan Chermayeff, is in Franklin Gothic. It appears on all museum letterheads and signage. The same studio also designed the Summergarden logo for the free evening concert programme.

Bags for the museum shop, designed by Takenobu Igarashi, draw their inspiration from two very different sources. The black, grey and white bag, which comes in several sizes, is criss-crossed with a mechanical-style black screen, a reference to computer graphics. The other bags are decorated by a

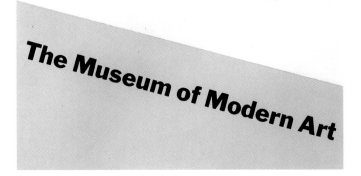

A range of stationery and admission tickets. The admission tickets carry the cropped, narrow version of the museum's name, suitable for vertical spaces.

MOMA's logo is set in Franklin Gothic. Designed by Chermayeff & Geismar Associates, it appears on a wide variety of materials produced by the museum, from letterheads to signage.

This page: two series of bags for the museum shop by the Japanese designer Takenobu Igarashi. *Above right*: a monochrome pattern inspired by computer graphics (1984); *right*: two bold colourways of a design in the contrasting style of spontaneous free-hand painting (1988). The colour is applied like a vigorous brush-stroke. Both sets of bags bear the museum's name prominently in Franklin Gothic.

free-hand splash in a single colour, like an over-sized brush-stroke. In both cases, the museum name is printed in Franklin Gothic.

Among the occasions for which an outside designer was commissioned is 'High & Low! Modern Art and Popular Culture', an exhibition exploring the relationship between the individual artistic imagination and the sometimes conflicting world of popular and commercial culture this century (on show at the museum from autumn 1990 to early 1991). Steven Schoenfelder selected a Constructivist typographic style, and drew upon the minimalist look of daily newspapers. His logo was based on a book cover by Alexander Rodchenko, dating from 1923, which was actually included in the exhibition. The highly legible retro-typography gives a singular identity to the visuals, which are picked up and adapted extremely well to all the exhibition documents.

MUSEUM OF MODERN ART, NEW YORK

This page: the museum's permanent image. The basic information booklet, where visitors can find a floorplan of the exhibition areas, provides a further example of the vertical-style logotype.

The museum commissions external graphic designers to work on temporary exhibitions. *Below* and *opposite*: Steven Schoenfelder's image for the 1990–91 exhibition, 'High & Low', which explored the relationship between modern art and advertising. The logo is based on a book cover (1923) by Alexander Rodchenko.

HIGH & LOW
MODERN ART AND POPULAR CULTURE

The exhibition is sponsored by AT&T

The Museum of Modern Art · New York

O C T O B E R   7 ,   1 9 9 0   —   J A N U A R Y   1 5 ,   1 9 9 1

An indemnity for the exhibition has been received from the Federal Council on the Arts and the Humanities.

The Organization of the Exhibition

PART I OF THE EXHIBITION, on the ground floor, addresses modern art's engagement with the broad field of Advertising, which includes newspapers, sales catalogues, and store windows, as well as magazine ads and billboards, up to about 1968. Part II, on the lower level, examines the relationships between modern artists and Graffiti, Caricature, and Comics, and concludes with a section devoted to contemporary art. (See the floor plans on the back page.) The internal history of each field — the way modern advertising developed, or comic strips and comic books evolved — is represented selectively, by examples chosen to illuminate their dialogue with modern painting and sculpture.

A Wheel, Not a Ladder

GIVE AND TAKE

THE TERMS "HIGH" AND "LOW" might be taken to imply a rigid hierarchy, arranged up and down like the rungs of a ladder. However, in studying the way certain forms and styles circulate between the smaller-audience world of avant-garde and the broader-audience world of popular culture, what we really find is a revolving interchange — a process that transfers things from one to a "high" position and back again, in a circular, wheel-like pattern. An object of common commerce — such as the crude cut of typefaces in the ads Schwitters clipped for his collages (p. 3) or the little printing dots in the comics Lichtenstein selected (p. 13) — taken out of the flow of everyday currency into a special, more prominent place in art; and then, through the action of that art, the same symbols return, somewhat transformed and with a new meaning — like the refined sans-serif typefaces of fashion magazines in the 1930s, or the prominent dots in pseudo-"Pop" advertisements today — into the broader world of popular culture.

This wheel has been kept in motion by a series of artists, typographers, commercial draftsmen, designers, publishers, and so on, each "picking the pocket" of the other in a roundel of borrowings and redistributions. And while its turnings hold the threat that things of great complexity and provocation may become trivialized into a bland currency, the wheel also shows again and again how art forms of great intensity and broad effect may be made from what might seem only the dross of everyday experience. The interworkings of society and art in our era seem to bear out a surprising aphorism: nothing so sacred that it may not be profaned, but nothing so profane that it may not be made, in a sense, sacred.

A Century Old and Still Evolving

The Dialogue Between Modern Art and Popular Culture

AROUND 1890 THE Post-Impressionist artist Georges Seurat, intent on finding a way to evoke the experience of the modern city, brought figures and styles from contemporary advertising posters into his paintings. His openness to inspiration from the styles and imagery of the street foreshadowed a new aspect of modern art — one that emerged full-blown just before World War I, when Pablo Picasso and other artists pasted scraps of newspapers and commercial wrappers into their works. From then on, direct borrowings from everyday ephemera gave artists a special way to confront the look and feel of modern society. And these borrowings — from ads, labels, signboards, shop windows, cheap magazines, and other commonplace sources — joined with new forms of abstraction to compound the challenges early modern art posed to conventional ways of thinking about painting and sculpture.

Through the ensuing decades and up to the present, modern art has expanded its openness to a changing popular culture; and the innovations of modern art have in turn rebounded back into that culture. In this traffic special bridges have been created, between the individual imaginations of artists and the public life of our epoch. "High and Low: Modern Art and Popular Culture" examines some of the most important of these connections.

A Vast Topic Seen in a Particular Focus

The avant-garde's inspirations from vernacular sources, and the complementary influence of vanguard artists on popular visual culture, offer a rich subject for study in diverse fields of modern creativity, including architecture, photography, music, and many others. To focus its exploration, this exhibition concentrates just on painters and sculptors. And it deals primarily with artists who worked in Paris and New York, though it includes works from other European countries and the Soviet Union.

The exhibition is not just concerned with *what* modern art showed — that is, with the countless cases in which artists have depicted such obvious motifs from popular culture as billboards or movie stars. Nor does it set out to chart modern artists' frequent use of "low" materials such as junk metal. "High and Low" emphasizes instead *how* modern art has been made: its central subject is the concrete, visible ways in which artists' innovative styles have been affected by (and in turn affected) aspects of popular culture.

What Does 'Popular Culture' Mean?

"Popular culture" is only a provisional term of convenience, used here to designate the world of commercial publicity, printed ephemera, pulp images, and illicit writing on public walls. "Popular" does not mean that these things are necessarily democratic in their origins or universally well-liked. And many areas that might be called "popular" art in other contexts — folk painting, for example, or children's drawings, or decorative kitsch — are not included. This show instead deals with more "streetwise" aspects of the visual culture associated with modern city life; and it specifically examines four major categories: Advertising, Graffiti, Caricature, and Comics.

Two of these areas, Advertising and Comics, are frequently associated with what is called "mass culture" or the "culture industry," because they involve things produced industrially and sold by mercantile corporations. Graffiti and Caricature, by contrast, are usually associated with more spontaneous, individual (if often anonymous) protest and social criticism. At any given moment everything within these categories may seem to be wholly "low," and firmly beneath the higher aspirations of art. But modern artists have, as the exhibition shows, constantly worked to subvert, rearrange, and sometimes transpose such hierarchies.

Particular Things and People

This exhibition's organizing ideas and themes are explained on text panels in the display, and in its accompanying publications (listed on p. 15). But its principal focus is on particular objects and people. Throughout the show, pairings of artists offer the opportunity to assess how individual temperaments have found, within the play between high and low, the possibilities for widely varying kinds of art: Kurt Schwitters and Aleksandr Rodchenko built on contrasting potentials of the printed word (p. 3); Fernand Léger and Marcel Duchamp discovered separate potentials in shop display (p. 5); Roy Lichtenstein and Philip Guston drew widely different styles and emotions from the world of comics (pp. 12-13); and Jeff Koons and Elizabeth Murray, by pursuing the dialogue of modern art and popular culture in almost opposite directions (p. 14), have continued to expand the range that this confrontation offers to the imaginations of individual creators.

This publication was printed by *The Star-Ledger*, Newark, New Jersey.

The Museum of Modern Art

HIGH & LOW

MODERN ART
POPULAR CULTURE

October 7, 1990–January 15, 1991

A major exhibition addressing the relationship between modern art and advertising, graffiti, caricature, and comics

Sponsored by AT&T
An indemnity for the exhibition has been received from the Federal Council on the Arts and the Humanities.

For information, call (212) 708-9850.

Evening Openings for Museums
New York

Designer **Alan Peckolick**
Work done **Poster**
Year **1984–85**

Mobil financed free openings on Tuesday evenings at certain New York museums: the Guggenheim, the Whitney Museum and the Museum of American Folk Art. Alan Peckolick was commissioned to design a poster to advertise the late openings.

The poster is typographic in content and austerely simple in design, using only upper case letters in various sizes. By increasing the size of the 'M's which begin and end the word 'museum', the designer creates a focused space for 'free' and 'Tues.', two of the primary pieces of information the poster is required to convey. The typography itself becomes a pictorial space. 'Free' and

'Tues.' also demand attention because of their striking colour, scarlet, which provides a link with the third important piece of information, 'evenings': people will be able to visit the museums after work. The museums are differentiated by varying the shade of blue used for each, from dark to mid- to pale blue.

The colours play another important role in addition to assisting the reader to assimilate the information quickly. Blue and red are the corporate colours of Mobil, whose contribution is acknowledged at the bottom of the poster by a reference to their grant and by their logo.

Alan Peckolick's poster to advertise late openings of three New York museums relies on typography and colour for its impact. Brilliant scarlet is employed to make the most important information leap out instantly ('free' and 'Tuesday evenings'), while the museums are linked by the use of blue, but separated by their differing shades. At the same time, blue and scarlet, Mobil's corporate colours, refer to the event's sponsor. The poster's very simplicity is a sophisticated technique for conveying information swiftly and clearly.

Siggraph is the annual computer graphics trade show and conference of the Association for Computing Machinery (ACM). Each year it is held at a different place in the United States. The event lasts for three or four days and attracts such luminaries of computer animation as George Lucas, Cranston Surrey and Robert Able.

In 1986, the venue was the gigantic Dallas Convention Center in Texas. Woody Pirtle was asked to develop a total graphics programme for all the directional and environmental signs; printed material such as stationery and catalogues; and promotional items including mugs and T-shirts. It was decided to symbolize graphically the conference location with a computer-generated flowering cactus image.

Ron Scott, a computer-buff photographer, was commissioned to work on the cactus motif. His high-resolution, computer-generated images were then broken down, and a pixelized central square of curved and zigzag shapes was incorporated into the design. The prickly pear image was used on an announcement poster, and different graphic elements and colours of the design were used on registration material and tickets, coursework books and catalogues for the computer art show.

The graphic design elements were also applied to the exterior and interior of the Convention Center. The dark tinted-glass façade was brightened with

ACM Siggraph
Dallas

Designer **Pentagram: Woody Pirtle**
Work done **Signage, stationery, promotional products**
Year **1986**

strips of coloured paper, while a Siggraph banner 100 feet wide (about 30 metres) was draped from the roof. In the lobby, a specially commissioned decorative carpet (60 feet/18 metres square) was laid, to work in conjunction with the signage banners. It also made the formidable scale of the space seem more human. The modular design, based on standard 24-inch-square (about 60 cm) carpet tiles, was an inventive solution to a tight budget constraint.

The promotional and identity programme is highly creative. While relying on computer images, it successfully keeps its own particular style, a highly contemporary quality of plasticity. The combination of photograph and computer graphics is especially relevant to the theme of the event.

Below left: poster with the cactus motif, a combination of photography and computer graphics, which was chosen to symbolize Texas. *Below*: merchandise with fragmented elements of the computer-generated image.

AUSTRALIA

The Powerhouse Museum is partially housed in the old Ultimo Power Station. The buildings, until recently derelict, are of sturdy industrial construction and contain a number of awe-inspiring spaces. The architectural shell was refurbished by the New South Wales government's Public Works Department, a complex process which combined major renovations with new building work.

The museum's collection contains more than 350,000 objects spanning the fields of science, technology, social history, the decorative arts and design. Several theatres provide programmes of film, music, drama and dance.

Emery Vincent Associates began by preparing a graphics brief, working with the primary consulting exhibition designer and museum staff. The idea for the logo was strongly inspired by the museum building and by its eclectic mixture of old and new constructions – the combination of metal and reinforced concrete. Architectural drawings, reduced to linear abstractions, make up the symbol which can be used either in its entirety or in fragments. In the latter case, it successfully retains its impact and visual flavour. In addition, a logo consisting of the name POWERHOUSE was created for use by itself on signs or as a caption to accompany the symbol.

The decorative nature of the symbol leads the visitor to give priority to reading the logo, which is easy to remember because it is simply the museum's name. The colours used have a warm, human feel, but they do not appear to be

Powerhouse Museum
Sydney

Designer **Emery Vincent Associates: Garry Emery**
Work done **Permanent signage, exhibition labelling system, stationery, merchandise**
Year **1987**

coded to strengthen the identity. Instead, they are simply taken from the building itself.

The basic visual identity has been applied by the museum to operational stationery, promotional and advertising materials and signage. The designers also developed an extensive hierarchical communications system to direct visitors around the building and to inform them about the museum's exhibitions of its vast and disparate collection. Computer-based information centres designed for the active participation of visitors were incorporated to assist with directions and thematic details of exhibitions.

The Powerhouse identity, determinedly contemporary in style, would have benefited from being honed down to the essentials.

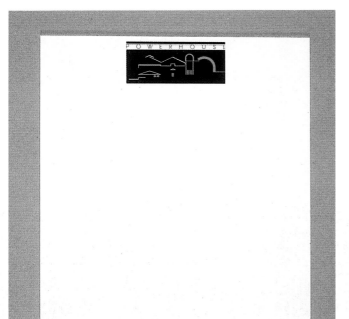

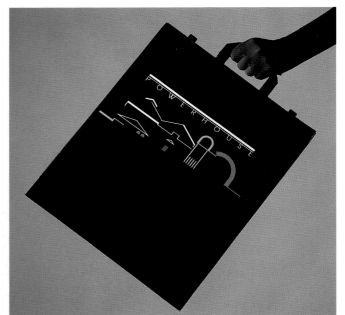

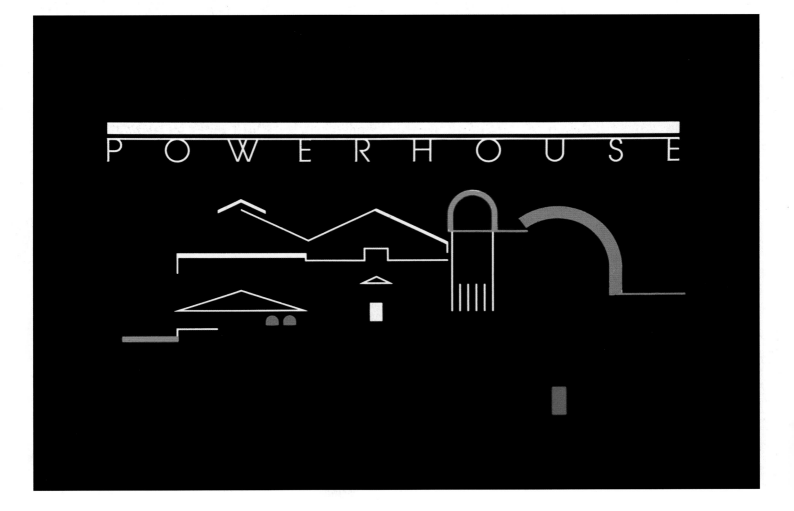

POWERHOUSE MUSEUM

The museum's symbol (*opposite, below*) consists of an abstracted diagrammatic representation of the building in which it is housed: compare the graphic symbol with the museum's exterior (*page 47* and *below*). It is supported by a name plate spelling out POWERHOUSE. Both components can be used separately, as seen above the museum's main entrance (*below*).

The museum has found a vast range of applications for its distinctive mark, ranging from stationery to shopping bags (*opposite*), T-shirts and umbrellas. Although the graphic mark is used for exterior signage, it is not featured on internal directional signs or the labelling system.

Australian Bicentennial Celebrations
Throughout Australia

Designer Cato Design: Ken Cato
Work done Alphabet, urban signage
Year 1987–88

Australia's two-hundredth birthday, celebrated on 26 January 1988, was marked by about 2,000 events organized all over the country from the end of 1987 and on through 1988. The events were designed to have a wide appeal: for instance, a visit by a flotilla of Tall Ships to Australian ports; international cricket; a wheelbarrow team race. The arts were also widely represented by a whole range of activities: an exhibition of contemporary Aboriginal art; an exhibition of Tasmanian art; a performing arts summer school for young people; a country music festival; an exhibition of 100 years of posters.

A national competition was held to select a symbol for the bicentenary and the winning entry was a stylized map of Australia. Cato – who was not the designer of the map – was then commissioned to design an alphabet (complete with numbers) to reflect the winning symbol's characteristics. Cato's typeface appeared prominently on the large celebration banners which adorned the streets of Australia's major cities – one application among many.

Of his typeface, the most frequently used components were the numerals making up the bicentenary date, which was reduced to '88'. Each '8' is divided into three oblique areas, which produces the effect of brilliantly coloured streaks: green, red and yellow against a royal blue background. Minimalist and highly typographic in style, the abbreviated date was employed not only on the street banners, but also appeared on numerous commercial items.

The celebration banners also carried the winning map symbol, the text 'Australia 1788–1988' in Univers and large-scale illustrations of figures such as Captain Cook and an Aborigine. The portraits, also designed by Cato, are treated as outline drawings, in monochrome or two colours – red or blue and white, highlighted with yellow. Their graphic technique recalls that of the 'Mai 68' posters in France; the economical means of expression unleashes a powerful street-image.

The whole graphic ensemble was in keeping with the activities which made up the celebrations and fitted in with public expectations, bringing together perfectly the historical and contemporary aspects of the occasion.

Street banners, hung out in Australia's major cities, to celebrate the bicentenary of its discovery by Captain Cook.

Opposite: a striking street-image is created by Cato's pictorial street banners, with their bold portraits of Captain Cook and an Aborigine.

Right: typographic, minimalist-style banners proclaim '88', which stands for both the year of Cook's arrival (1788) and the bicentenary year (1988). The numbers are part of the typeface commissioned from Ken Cato to accompany the winning entry in a competition to find a symbol for the anniversary – a stylized map of Australia.

Sailmaker Gallery
Port Adelaide

Designer Barrie Tucker Design Pty Ltd: Barrie Tucker (art director);
Carolyn Tilly (designer, finished art)
Work done Stationery, invitations
Year 1986

The Sailmaker Gallery is a privately run commercial gallery, established in 1986 in a designated 'heritage' area of Port Adelaide, alongside the South Australian Maritime Museum. The buildings there are among the oldest in South Australia and are of great historical and architectural interest. The gallery is no exception, as it occupies a former sailmaker's brick loft dating from the 1860s. Originally, the building was one floor lower than it is today: what is now the cellar was once the ground floor, but because of water seepage and flooding from the Port River, a whole area of land was filled in the late nineteenth century. Among the building's interesting architectural details are colonial bond brickwork and solid River Red Gum beams from which sails were hung whilst being mended.

The Sailmaker Gallery specializes in items with a maritime theme, including paintings, limited-edition prints, ceramics and carved wooden pieces by local craftspeople.

The gallery's graphics are inspired by the basic building blocks of the Swiss school: knowing how to put together an original and relevant composition from simple geometric shapes, such as the circle, square and triangle. Colours, positioning, materials, textures, all form a part of the graphic design which must, in addition, give a meaning to the functional image. The text is reversed out against a dark blue background in strips, rather like DYMO (sticky-backed strips embossed with letters). The prominent incorporation of a triangle into the graphics evokes a ship's sail, and hence the name of the gallery. Several variations on the sail imagery are created either by using paper cut-outs or by folding the paper.

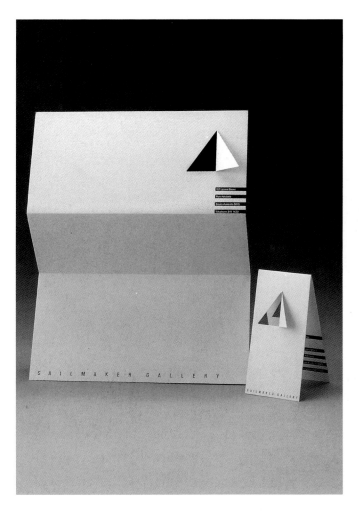

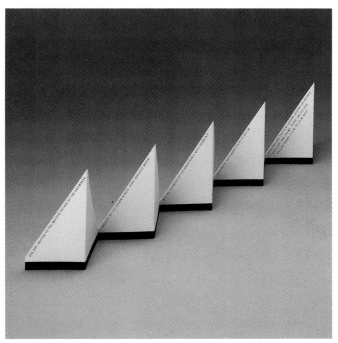

The graphics are inspired by the Swiss school and make use of simple geometrical shapes, with a simple colour scheme: white paper, black and royal blue. The nautical flavour is emphasized by triangular 'sails' and sea-blue address blocks.

Stationery (*left*) and invitations to the gallery's opening.

The Melbourne International Festival of the Arts began life in 1986 as the Melbourne Spoleto Festival. By the time it changed its name in 1990, it had already evolved into an event with world-wide recognition; attendance figures for 1990 (675,000) were double those for 1989. The festival, held each year in spring (September), celebrates the world's best opera, dance, music, drama, literature, film and design. Many events are free. It is run by a permanent staff and funded by the Ministry for the Arts and private sponsors.

The concept of the Spoleto Festival symbol was based on the traditional theatre mask, treated in a contemporary fashion. A three-dimensional model of the mask was created, then set alight and photographed from different angles for use as the main image on promotional material. It became the theme linking all components of the festival and has since been artistically reinterpreted through other media. Through the use of photography, painting, drawing and collage, the designer is able to fit the idea of the mask with considerable vitality to the needs of all the festival's support material. On the 1990 poster, for instance, a photograph of a mask is set in an Expressionist ambiance à la Murnau, amid collage and hand-written and typeset lettering. This same variety in treatment is echoed in the Melbourne Spoleto street banners (1989), where the mask appears in solid colours. On the black and white-speckled programme folders, the mask appears as a stencil, produced in a spontaneous hand-drawn

Melbourne International Festival of the Arts
Melbourne

Designer **Cato Design: Ken Cato**
Work done **Logo, signage, printed matter**
Year **1989–90**

style, and is backed up by a typographic text. A splash of a single bright colour, including yellow and red, shows through a window in the standard folder designed to contain event information.

The range of documents as a whole is lively and good at conveying information, its manner of communication seductive. The identity would, however, benefit from reducing its methods of expression.

The poster for the 1990 Melbourne International Festival of the Arts. The image is a variation on the festival's permanent symbol of a theatrical mask.

The range of colours employed is sober: black for the typography, enlivened by red ('M' and 'International') and yellow/orange ('Melbourne International Festival'); black, grey, dark blue and white for the background and the photographic mask, made vivid by red-tinted eyes; and brown/purple and black for the stencil mask.

MELBOURNE INTERNATIONAL FESTIVAL OF THE ARTS

A selection of material designed to promote the 1989 event, its last
year as the 'Melbourne Spoleto Festival' (*this page* and *opposite*).

Below: the main festival poster on a wall in a Melbourne street. The
symbol is an amalgam of a photograph of a model of a mask that was
actually set alight and of a hand-painted stencil. *Right*: the programme
cover, with a further variation on the burning mask/stencil image.

The stencil image appears in its simplest form on the standard programme folder designed to contain event information (*above*). A window lets the title and vivid colours of the individual programme show through.

Street banners also carry the stencil image, this time its bright, hand-painted form (*right*), which is echoed in the colours of the decorative bunting.

FRANCE

The nucleus of the Louvre's enormous store of treasures is the art collection accumulated over the years by the kings of France. Despite a proposal put forward in the reign of Louis XVI (1774–92) that the royal collection should be exhibited to the public, nothing came of this until 1793 under the Convention, when the 'Central Museum of Arts' was instituted by decree. As the years went on, the museum continued to expand until by 1983 it occupied three-fifths of the former royal Palais du Louvre.

Before Ieoh Ming Pei was commissioned in 1983 to build an extension, the result of which was the Pyramide, the museum came to seem more and more cramped and antiquated with each passing year. Pei's project had to fulfil three objectives. It had to make better provision for visitors; to increase space for exhibiting the collections and for the reserves; and to develop the technical services necessary for the management and security of a modern museum.

Pei's Pyramide creates an interior space bathed in light. The Hall Napoléon, which extends beneath the transparent structure, is treated in a manner that is strongly graphic. Its most important features are the play between line and plane, black and white, light and shade. It is the bringing together of quite different materials – glass, steel, concrete, stone – that creates the extreme sobriety of the decor, which is devoid of all colour except that of the ever-changing Parisian sky. The trees which grow inside, lining the approaches to the

Louvre
Paris

Designer **Atelier de Création Graphique – Grapus**
Work done **Logo, stationery, publications**
Year **1989**

Richelieu, Denon and Sully Pavilions beneath each 'pyramidion', highlight the close relationship between nature and architecture.

The opening of the Hall Napoléon is the first stage of the Grand Louvre project, due for completion in 1993, the museum's bicentenary year. Its expansion into space occupied until 1989 by the Ministère des Finances means that the Louvre will offer an extraordinary concentration of exhibits at one site.

In 1988, the Centre National des Arts Plastiques (part of the Ministère de la Culture) launched a competition to find a graphic design studio to create a new visual identity system for the museum. The international jury presided over by I.M. Pei chose Grapus's entry. They were offered a one-year contract to design and produce a logo, stationery and publishing concept.

The logotype is a rectangular panel in which the word 'Louvre' is printed. The initial 'L' is noticeably larger than the other letters; all are reversed out against sky with floating clouds. An imposing, stately impression is introduced by accentuating the space between the letters, like an inscription on a monument, while the use of the 17th-century typeface Granjon expresses the Louvre's historical legacy.

LOUVRE

The Louvre's logotype is a sophisticated design product, sufficiently flexible to be suitable for use in numerous contexts. It appears on the institution's facade, on all its stationery and publications and on its merchandise.

A selection of printed material, all carrying the logo. *Opposite* : illustrated guidebook (*above*) and publicity folder for the opening of the auditorium (*below*). *Above* : orientation plans in Italian, Spanish and Japanese. *Right* : invitations to conferences.

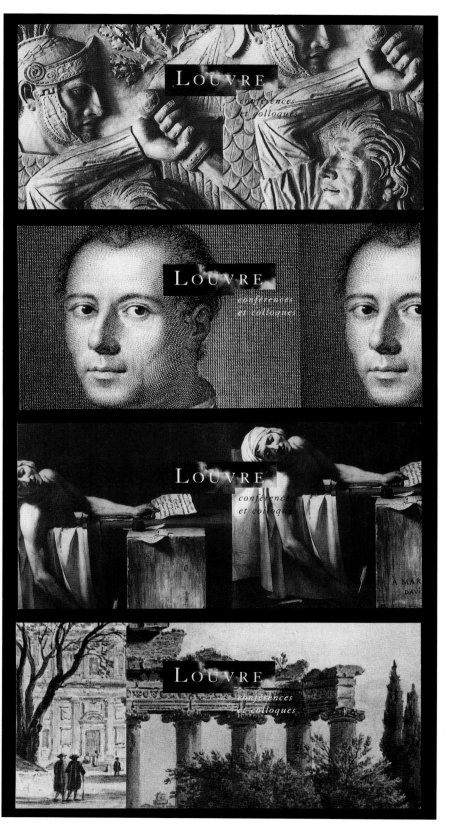

In creating the logo, Grapus first of all abandoned 'Musée du Louvre' in favour of the simple, more hieratic 'Louvre'. They kept, however, the 17th-century typeface Granjon for the museum's name, which is printed in upper case against a background of sky with clouds. Granjon captures the spirit of the Louvre's history and its collections, while the sky evokes the Pyramide's transparency. Despite its simplicity the background of sky makes it quite difficult to reproduce the logo.

Grapus summarize the conceptual basis of the logo in the design standards manual: 'The logotype consists of a rectangular panel in which "Louvre" is printed in Granjon, the initial letter appreciably larger than its fellows. The letter-spacing is accentuated in the manner of engravings on monumental façades. The lettering is reversed out against the sky enlivened by light clouds. The logo expresses the tensions between permanence and mobility, between history and art, between time and space, and derives its strength from vital contradictions.'

The titles and subheadings of information documents are set in Univers, a typeface which reflects the Louvre's modern identity. The typography for publications is in Granjon.

LOUVRE

A selection of stationery for use by various departments of the museum; all bear the logo with its cloud motif. The envelope (*right*) is particularly witty. The text is punctuated by people in silhouette, who cast shadows of words.

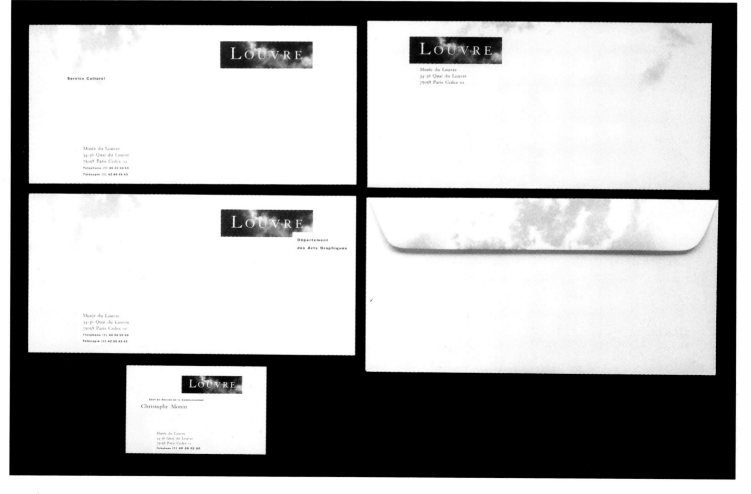

LOUVRE

The museum communicates details of temporary and one-off events by a variety of means. *Left*: assorted programmes for workshops and conferences. *Below*: a three-monthly activities programme and a poster for a temporary exhibition about people who have donated items to the museum.

Banner hanging outside the museum.

The Louvre's logotype suffers from one disadvantage: despite the visual simplicity of the lettering against the sky, the logotype is technically difficult to reproduce. This sometimes leads to a loss of definition, especially in the clouds.

Agence pour la Promotion de la Création Industrielle (A.P.C.I.)
Paris

Designer Tout pour Plaire
Work done Visual identity system, including stationery, posters, programmes, press releases, brochure
Year 1983

A.P.C.I. was set up in 1983 by the Ministère de la Culture to encourage new industrial design and promote existing contemporary design. Its areas of concern are graphic, product and environmental design, as well as fashion. It functions as a catalyst in the generation of ideas, working with different partners for each new project in which it participates. A.P.C.I.'s own team is small but it takes on specialists according to the requirements of specific ventures. New designs are stimulated by competitions which bring together designers and manufacturers. These help to establish the designers' reputations and to spur industry to action, which in turn leads to new markets for both parties. Existing design is promoted through books, exhibitions, television programmes and awards. A.P.C.I.'s bi-monthly journal, *Design Chronique*, is a condensation of the professional press which enables designers to stay abreast of current developments in the industry.

Tout pour Plaire's visual identity system contains neither logotype nor monogram. Instead, the design concept is communicated through the use of blocks of primary colours, printed solid. Consciously abstract and non-representational, it conveys a sense of 'pure design'. It has a dynamic presence that commands recognition through its use of colour combined with basic rectangular shapes. The sober typography gives it a contemporary feel.

The journal, whose first issue appeared in 1988, was designed by Michaël Levin deliberately to clash with the visual identity. Stylistically, his design belongs to the Neville Brody school. Six pages, two colours (red and black), and typography that is austere and 'retro' are brought together to achieve a harmonious visual effect.

A.P.C.I.'s visual identity achieves recognition through the use of the three primary colours, red, yellow and blue, and its three basic rectangles (which can be manipulated to become related geometric shapes). The organization successfully communicates its goal – design – through its non-representational image.

A range of printed material shows the basic colour blocks and variations on the theme. *Below*: cover (back and front) of a booklet introducing A.P.C.I. and its objectives.

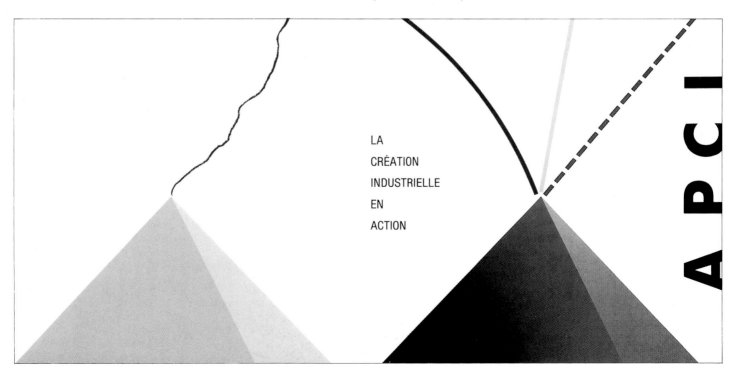

LA
CRÉATION
INDUSTRIELLE
EN
ACTION

A P C I

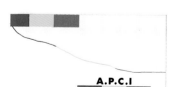

Left and *above*: letterhead, correspondence and visiting cards; 'Perspectives 86', an annual programme, folds into a neat square (*below left*); and a large booklet on A.P.C.I. and its activities (*below*).

La Villette
Paris

Designer **Grapus 83, Grapus 86, Grapus 87**
Work done **Logo, visual identity manual, journal**
Year **1983; 1986–87**

La Villette is an extensive park covering about 125 acres (50 hectares). Its function is new for a park; providing a home for a broad range of cultural organizations – the Cité des Sciences et de l'Industrie, the Cité de la Musique and the Grande Halle – under the umbrella of a single institution – the Etablissement Public de la Villette. There are several constructions in the park: the Musée des Sciences, designed by Adrien Fainsilber; the Grande Halle, by H. Janvier, renovated in 1986 by Robert and Reichen; the Cité de la Musique by Christian de Portzamparc; and Bernard Tschumi's Parc Urbain.

Clearly so diverse a complex needed a visual unifier to make the public aware that it was in fact a single entity. Grapus had to find solutions to the problems created by the need for a graphic identity that would remain coherent over a vast physical expanse and that would unite harmoniously such different cultural activities.

Grapus's graphics draw upon simple geometric shapes, together with a 'typewritten' typographic style. The visuals are in the hand-drawn tradition and are used largely in conjunction with photographs.

The graphics system is complex but logical. First of all, there is a logotype to represent La Villette as a single entity. That is, the physical area made up of three distinct institutions: the Parc de la Villette, symbolized by a green inverted triangle; the Cité des Sciences et de l'Industrie, symbolized by a red square; and the Cité de la Musique, symbolized by a blue circle. This logotype is used by La Villette for all its communications as an institution and for the general operations of the site as a whole. The basic logotype can be varied so that it refers to each of La Villette's constituent institutions by retaining the relevant geometric symbol in colour while reproducing the others in black.

The logotype can either be set within a rectangular panel outlined in black or stand alone. The panel is in the ratio 3:1 and can be positioned either horizontally or vertically. The logotype for La Villette appears alone within its panel, but in the case of the variations to represent the individual organs, the institution's name appears as well. The typeface is Gill Bold 2128 (Berthold

catalogue reference). Lower case letters only are used, except for the first letter of proper nouns. The definite article must be included. The design standards manual, published in 1985, sets out clearly the different approaches to be taken in different situations: for audiovisuals, published documents, printed material to be read from a distance, press releases.

In 1986, a logo was commissioned for the Grande Halle. An elongated grey or silver cow, it is better known than that of La Villette and is in fact sometimes thought of as the logo for the other institutions. The style of the logo succeeds in establishing a relationship between the shape of the animal's body and the structure of the building – a vast span supported by rows of metal girders like ribs. The image of the cow is a reminder of the Halle's former use as an abattoir, but also represents its transformation into a place where arts, sciences and leisure activities come together – the cow in search of green pastures supplies us with an unceasing stream of cultural experiences. The green triangle – or 'V' – positioned as an asterisk shows that the Grande Halle is attached to the Parc de la Villette. The cow faces in the direction the reader's eye should travel – generally towards the right. Texts are printed in Gill.

La Villette's identity is intelligent and intellectually rich in its conception. The very complexity of its application means that there is still enough space for a certain amount of breaking of the rules and for the whims of future presidents.

La Villette's visual identity is a complex but eminently logical solution to the problems presented by an organization which unites many diverse components. The logotype of the federal institution – La Villette – can be subtly altered to represent the individual bodies within it, as illustrated by the range of printed material opposite.

Below and right: **the memorable elongated cow of the Grande Halle is a reminder of the building's original use as an abattoir. Although part of the Parc de la Villette (indicated by the green triangle, or 'V', beside the cow and by the green 'V' of 'Villette' on the poster), it is often mistakenly perceived as the symbol of La Villette as a whole.**

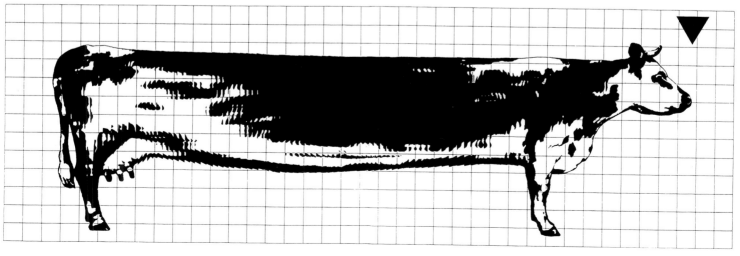

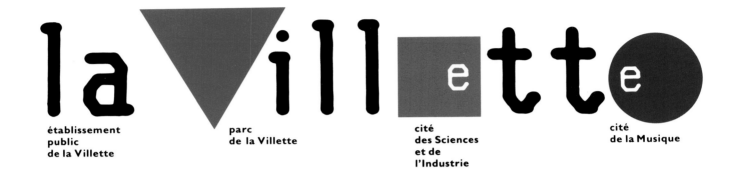

<table>
<tr>
<td>établissement
public
de la Villette</td>
<td>parc
de la Villette</td>
<td>cité
des Sciences
et de
l'Industrie</td>
<td>cité
de la Musique</td>
</tr>
</table>

Le logotype "la Villette" est décliné suivant quatre cas principaux:

triangle allumé en vert, le logotype la Villette représente le parc de la Villette.

carré allumé en rouge, le logotype la Villette représente la cité des Sciences et de l'Industrie.

cercle allumé en bleu, le logotype la Villette représente la cité de la Musique.

triangle allumé en vert, carré allumé en rouge, cercle allumé en bleu, c'est le logotype "la Villette" qu'utilise l'établissement public de la Villette (EPV) dans ses messages de communication institutionnelle et pour les opérations générales du Site.

Remarque : les trois formes géométriques dans leur couleur respective n'ont pas vocation individuelle de logotype ; les formes de base ne sont utilisées seules que dans le cas où elles ont valeur de point de repérage, d'astérisque, auprès des logotypes spécifiques des organismes rattachés à l'une des trois institutions majeures.
(cf : l'image de la géode).

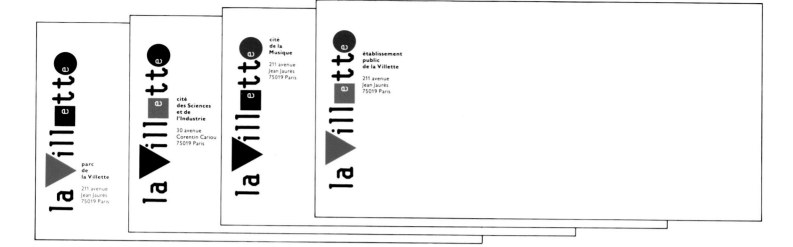

LA VILLETTE

There are exhaustive guides which set out the rules governing the complex visual identity and which provide clear examples of correct usage, to aid the people who must apply them to all the organization's activities (*right*).

Opposite, below: page from the design standards manual which explains how the basic logotype of La Villette as a whole (*bottom*) can be varied to represent its constituent entities; *above*: logotype with the appropriate setting of each body's name. *This page, above*: letterheaded paper for the Etablissement Public de la Villette and its subsidiary components.

Salon International de l'Architecture
Paris

Designer **Michel Quarez**
Work done **CAD graphics for use on posters, brochures, badges, etc.; exhibition graphics**
Year **1988, 1989, 1990**

The Salon International de l'Architecture is an annual event intended for both professionals and the general public. From its inauguration in 1986 until 1990 it took place in the Grande Halle of La Villette in Paris, but in 1991 the Salon was held in Milan, a reflection of its growing international recognition. Architectural projects are exhibited through the use of plans, models, videos and so on, over an area of about 1200 square yards (1000 square metres). Various meetings and debates are organized to discuss matters raised by the projects.

The high-quality graphics are printed in solid colour. The strong, computer graphics are perfect illustrations of the event's theme: a bird sitting on its nest (1988); a man shouldering a tool (1989); a man in motion (1990). When reduced for reproduction in black and white on badges, or on colourful enamelled pins, the vigour and machine-produced spirit of the image are even more apparent.

The influence of Tomaszewski and the Polish school can be detected in both the composition and the inseparability of text and image on the posters. The colours and the use of CAD have produced a graphic style that is strong, original and highly personal. This is a rare example of a creative graphic artist who has managed to avoid the pitfalls of computer graphics by working from an initial drawing, rather than starting from scratch on the computer, and by maintaining his distance from the machine, which is used merely as a tool.

Michel Quarez's images (1988–90) all make use of strong, computer-assisted graphics. Each illustrates its theme aptly and imaginatively. The three years are unified by their shared colours: fluorescent yellow, green, pinks and purple.

Centre National des Arts Plastiques (CNAP)
Paris

The Centre National des Arts Plastiques, one of the nine departments within the Ministère de la Culture, was set up in 1982. Its areas of responsibility are painting, sculpture, design, photography, crafts, etching and murals. Its principal mandates are currently public commissions, decisions on funding organizations throughout France, teaching and training, grants to artists, contemporary art centres and the Jeu de Paume. It also formulates national policy for acquisitions and promotional activities.

CNAP's logo, designed by Grapus, and the way it is used are meant to reflect directly painting and free-hand drawing. Its four-colour treatment allows a high-quality result when translating from colour to black and white and in reduction. The principle behind the stationery was to create an organizational chart showing the various departments: a difficult task because of the CNAP's hierarchical complexities. The 'Grapus style' can be seen in the union of idea and practical application: the use of primary colours, simple drawing, the use of free-hand graphics as a symbol of painting. The various publications, such as booklets and brochures, each use a different trick to catch the eye and arouse curiosity – sometimes at the expense of legibility. These items, such as the magazine *Arts Info*, are images that change, in contrast to the logo which remains fixed. The permanent logo with which the public is familiar and the succession of images join together in identifying CNAP.

Designers **Grapus 84 (corporate image). Roman Cieslewicz (annual reports 1988, 1989)**
Work done **Logo, stationery, fascia sign; magazines**
Year **1984; 1988–89**

It has been Grapus's policy to suggest other designers for certain documents: for instance, a different photographer for each issue of *Arts Info*. In addition, different graphic artists have designed the annual reports, which are built around some extremely striking photomontages. The annual reports for 1988 and 1989 by Roman Cieslewicz are particularly noteworthy – really books in their own right.

Although CNAP's visual identity initially attracted criticism, it has had – and indeed continues to have – considerable influence in French cultural circles.

Roman Cieslewicz's pages to introduce new chapters in CNAP's annual report for 1989 employ photomontage. The black and white is relieved by the fuchsia pink of the chapter numbers and corresponding arms.

ENSEIGNEMENT 1

INCITATION A LA CREATION 2

BICENTENAIRE 1789-1989 3

PROMOTION DIFFUSION 4

ENRICHISSEMENT DU PATRIMOINE 5

FONCTIONNEMENT 6

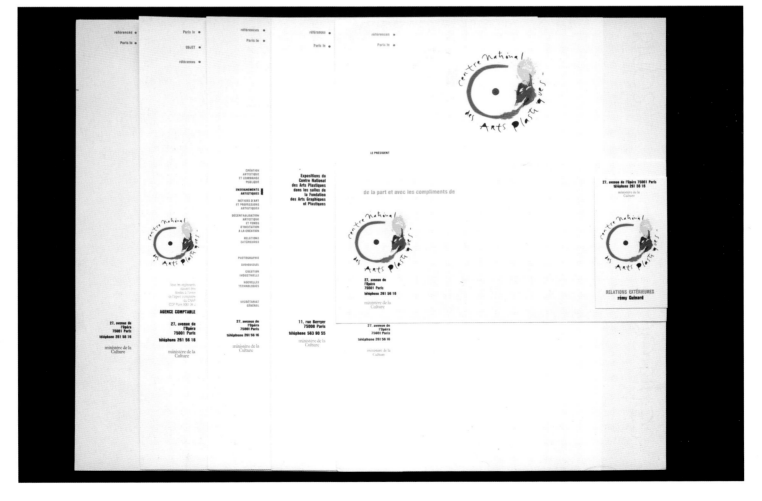

CENTRE NATIONAL DES ARTS PLASTIQUES

Grapus's logo (*opposite, above left*), with its hand-written letters and colourful free-hand drawing, has all the vivid immediacy of painting. It is the permanent, unchanging image of the organization, used, for instance, on stationery (*opposite*) and invitations to exhibitions (*right*). A succession of changing images, however, is created for CNAP's publications (*below*).

Ministère de la Culture
Paris

Designer Intégral Concept: Pippo Lionni
Work done Logo
Year 1989

The importance of the Ministère de la Culture is reflected in the size of its budget – one per cent of France's national budget. Its official title, 'Ministère de la Culture, de la Communication et des Grands Travaux', indicates its areas of concern: culture (art, theatre, design etc.); communications (audiovisual media); major public works (e.g. the Louvre extension). It is divided up into nine departments, as well as external services and public bodies.

The logo was intended to coordinate more fully the different aspects of the Ministère so as to achieve recognition of the whole as a unit. At the same time, no one area was to be favoured above the rest. Lionni explains the identity's framework as follows: 'The institutional identity system . . . is based on three fundamental principles. First, the logotype must be able to accommodate eventual changes in the official title of the Ministère (Bicentenaire has since been dropped). Secondly, the system must be open-ended and able to function well in all the situations where it is used – capable of balancing independence at a departmental level with centralization. Lastly, it must reflect the fact that the Ministère is a force for stimulating, sustaining and promoting cultural expression; it is the driving force behind and makes the decisions about all French cultural activities.'

The logo was first used on information documents; it is planned to extend it to stationery. Helvetica Light and Helvetica Black were selected for the typography because of their neutrality, versatility and legibility. Both upper and lower case letters are used, but never solely upper case. Contrasting background colours were chosen to make stand out as much as possible the words 'Ministère', 'Communication', 'Grands Travaux' and 'Bicentenaire', which are always white. 'Culture', however, is transparent, so that it takes on the colour or motif of the surface on which the logo is set. This transparency is crucial to the identity, as it creates an interaction between 'Culture' and the background on which it is placed. The background itself is drawn into being an integral part of the identity, while the logotype takes on a specific meaning in a given situation. The logotype panel is printed solid and never screened.

Lionni's logotype emphasizes the word 'Culture' in two ways: by its size and by extending it beyond the symbolic boundary of the panel. This overflow has a further important effect when combined with the transparency of the characters: both help to establish an interactive relationship between 'Culture' and the background against which it is placed. The background becomes an integral part of the identity.

Centre Georges Pompidou
Paris

The Centre Georges Pompidou opened its doors to the public in 1977. It was founded as a multidisciplinary organization – painting, sculpture, photography, literature, design and music – in four departments: the Musée d'Art Moderne (MAM), the Bibliothèque Publique d'Information (BPI), the Centre de Création Industrielle (CCI) and IRCAM (music department). As president has followed president, Widmer's original unifying identity and sign system for the Centre as a whole has been warped by a continuous process of change. The result has been graphic anarchy, without any rules or communications strategy. All that has survived is the symbol representing the building (Widmer and Ernst Hiestand, 1974). CCI has, however, escaped the general confusion and has built a strong visual identity around its publications, both institutional and related to temporary events.

The thematic exhibitions involving all four departments have sometimes given rise to interesting images. These extensive multimedia events, such as 'Paris-Berlin' (1978), 'Paris-Moscow' (1979), 'Paris-Paris' (1981), have brought together painting, sculpture, photography, design, architecture and music. Their contribution to the international success of the Centre has been considerable. The mixing of disciplines was strikingly innovative and reflected a desire to bring together literature, fine arts and music. In the 1990s, however, museums are debating whether to return to isolating the genres.

Designers **Visuel Design: Jean Widmer. Roman Cieslewicz**
Work done **Logo, posters, catalogue, invitations**
Year **1974, 1978–91**

A photographic approach, including photomontage, was adopted for the exhibition graphics by Roman Cieslewicz, a multi-talented graphic designer. The economy of means of his work diminishes neither the appositeness nor the coherence of his images. He draws his inspiration from Surrealist painting and photography. His humour can be black. His layouts and typography are always simple but well constructed. His posters have won international acclaim and are real works of pictorial art, provocative and irreverent. His work, whether posters, brochures or book jackets, always bears witness to the originality of an artist whose ideas are full of diversity, tension and sensitivity.

Roman Cieslewicz's banner in yellow and black for the 1981 multimedia exhibition 'Paris-Paris'.

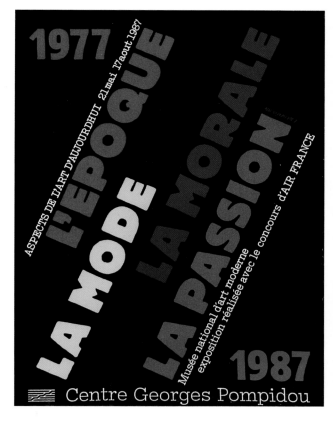

CENTRE GEORGES POMPIDOU

Opposite : posters for large thematic exhibitions in which the Centre's various departments participated. The images were repeated on the associated invitations and catalogues. The keynotes over the ten-year period (1979–89): strong typography, economy of means and relevance of the image to the event. (Designer: Roman Cieslewicz)

Right : poster for a 1991 design exhibition at the CCI. It is notable for the effective use of space made by its compact typography. The lettering runs vertically against a lively photograph. (Designer: Visuel Design: Jean Widmer, Laurent Ungerer)

CENTRE GEORGES POMPIDOU

The exterior of the building is used to advertise events. The poster for the 'Magiciens de la Terre' (1989) was designed by BBV and Peter Saville Associates (art directors, Ruedi Baus and Peter Saville; designer, Denis Coueignoux).

The innovative visual identity of the CCI, the Centre's design department, which has been created and developed by Visuel Design/Jean Widmer, has achieved a remarkable unity of style.

Visuel Design's strategy for CCI since 1987 has been faithfully followed and is used for all items – invitations, programmes, publications. It achieves a remarkable unity of style, that of Jean Widmer. The identity derives great power from its use of electric blue, four squares and Gill typeface; from its permanant formats, the wide variety of images (photos, montages, sketches, etc.) and its inventive yet rigorous typography. The equation of event, theme and medium is skilfully solved.

Raymond
LOEWY
un pionnier du design américain

Hélène Ahrweiler
Président du Centre national d'art
et de culture Georges Pompidou

François Burkhardt
Directeur du Centre de Création
Industrielle

vous prient de leur faire
le plaisir d'assister à
l'inauguration de l'exposition **Raymond Loewy :
un pionnier
du design américain**

le mardi 26 juin 1990
à 18h30
au Centre Georges Pompidou
Galerie du CCI
(mezzanine)

Exposition produite
par l'Internationales
Design Zentrum Berlin e.V.

Invitation pour deux personnes

Entrées : rue Beaubourg et
parc de stationnement du Centre

27 juin-24 septembre 1990

**Shown here:
exhibition invitations,
1989–91 (Visuel
Design: Jean Widmer).**

CAPC Musée d'Art Contemporain
Bordeaux

Designer Total Design: Daphne Duijvelshoff-van Peski
Work done Graphic communication and sign system
Year 1985

The CAPC Musée d'Art Contemporain was founded in 1984 on the initiative of the local mayor. Its objective: to redefine the relationship between contemporary art and the general public. It is housed in a dockside warehouse which was erected in 1824 and converted to its new use between 1984 and 1990. The sizable range of activities testifies to the fact that this is a living museum. Its permanent collection is being built up by commissioning international artists to design and produce works especially for its cathedral-like naves.

Jean-Louis Froment, the museum's creator and director, describes the intentions behind its graphics programme: 'Our logo is the universe' (a pun on 'universe' and the typeface Univers). 'I wanted our work itself to be the logo – that is, I wanted the emblem to suggest the content and distinctive features of our activities, to encapsulate the way in which all our work must take place within the actual structures of a museum.'

The solution adopted was to use the Univers typeface, designed by Adrian Frutiger, which is particularly suited to photocomposition techniques. All the different publications – cards, catalogues, information sheets, posters, folders and so on – are variations on a theme: the use of the Univers typeface creates a graphic trademark, reinforced by solid-printed colours which provide its only real identity system.

The administrative stationery is always printed in Univers in black and white on white 'Opale de Rives' paper. The only exception is the 'M' of 'Musée' which is printed blue in upper case. On the back of the envelope, all the Univers sorts are printed in sequence, along with the motto *Notre logo c'est l'Univers*. The colour scheme of the publications mirrors that of the building: greys, whites, brick and wood tones, lacquered metal tinged with yellow. Information documents for the public are laid out according to a grid in which the letters of the title are often only partly visible; as much as possible, without making them too difficult to read, is cropped.

In a decade dominated by image manipulation, this museum's bias towards minimalism produces graphics of notable quality and versatility.

CAPC's identity is built not upon pictorial images, but on the use of colour, printed solid, and the Univers typeface. *Right* and *opposite below*: front and back of a selection of invitations.

The museum's graphic trademark is the Univers typeface, always printed in black except for the 'M' of 'Musee', which can be either blue or grey. *Above*: detail of folder and of the two sides of the envelope. The museum's punning motto appears on the back of the envelope, and both items feature typeface characters printed in sequence.

Musée d'Orsay
Paris

Designers **Bruno Monguzzi and Visuel Design: Jean Widmer (competition winners). Later work – Jean Widmer, with Roberto Ostinelli, Gérard Plénacoste, Nicole Widmer.**
Work done **Sign system, visual identity**
Year **1986**

The museum is housed in the old Gare d'Orsay, which was designed in 1898 by Victor Laloux for the Exposition Universelle of 1900. Following the station's closure in 1975, a competition for architects was launched in 1979 at the request of the Direction des Musées de France, a department of the Ministère de la Culture. The winner was ACT (R. Bardon, P. Colboc, J.P. Philippon).

In 1980 the Italian architect Gae Aulenti was put in charge of fitting out the interior. The architecture of the museum draws on both past and present idioms and preserves behind the contemporary fittings Laloux's station, especially the massive 'nave'. It succeeds in marrying the different environments with a variety of top-quality materials.

The museum has adopted a multidisciplinary policy, built around the concept of a 'sequences collage': exhibits which would normally fall in different departments, for instance painting and sculpture, are displayed together in a chronological sequence. The absence of the usual division by departments creates juxtapositions which show to great advantage the artistic production of the second half of the nineteenth century.

The museum's graphic designers, Widmer and Monguzzi, won a competition in 1983 for the sign system. (The same team went on to devise the museum's visual identity, together with its institutional documents.) The fragmented spatial organization of the building created particular difficulties. Before putting forward any programme, the designers had to examine carefully the problems of orientation produced by the various open spaces and routes between them, in order to come up with the best response to the demands of a public building devoted to cultural activities.

To make the collection manageable for the visitor, the museum is organized into the following sections by the age and medium of the exhibits, from 1848 to 1914: painting; sculpture; architecture; Art Nouveau; early cinematography; and temporary exhibitions.

The orientation panel, in four languages, uses typography to suggest the most important and those of lesser importance among the museum's various

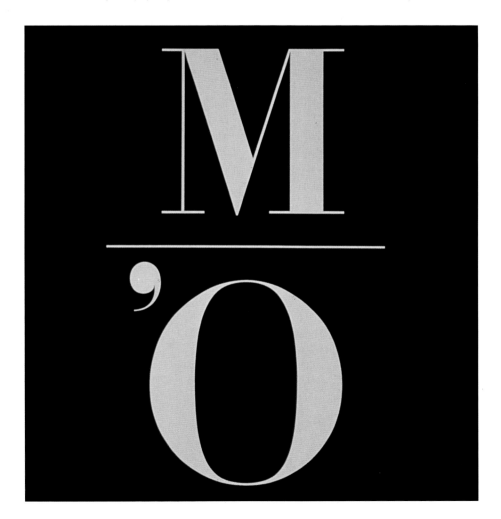

The museum's monogram consists of an 'M' above an 'O', separated by a fine rule, like two exposures on a reel of film. The selection of items opposite highlights its flexibility; it is often cropped in a variety of ways. Whether printed small (on a postage stamp) or large (on the 4½-yard/4-metre poster to mark the museum's opening in 1986), the monogram is perfectly readable.

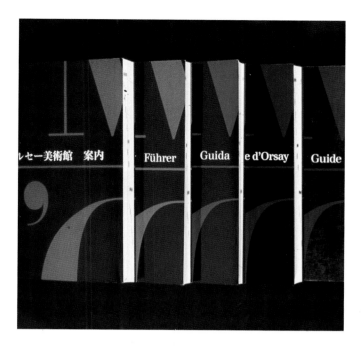

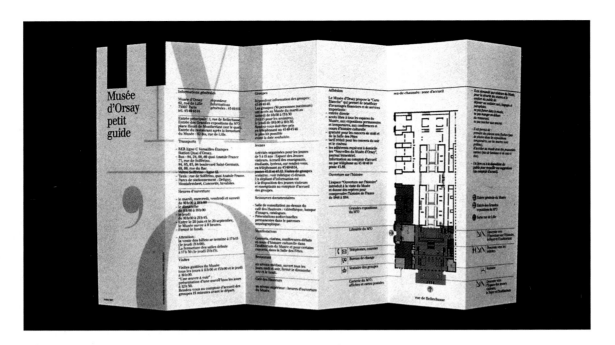

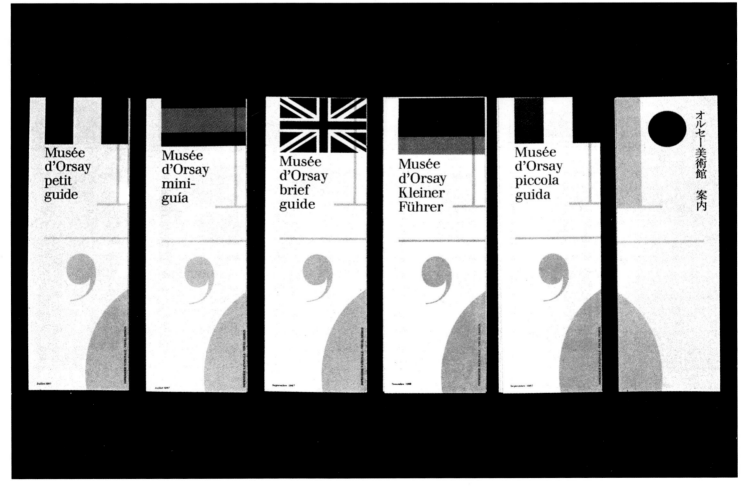

exhibits. The panels giving the names of the exhibition rooms are metallic and can be interchanged, as they slide into a brass frame. Parallel bars can be used to indicate directions.

Twelve 'key points', devoted to specific areas, are distributed around the museum to provide information and instruction. Here the visitor can sit down and consult the information sheets produced by the museum. These can be taken home and collected to make up a comprehensive history of art. The 'key points' are marked on a floor-plan which shows their location and indicates the subjects covered. A video screen informs visitors of daily events.

The labels for the exhibits are composed on films which are directly screened in red lacquer and set on black-lacquered metal. Recorded information is given in five languages (French, English, German, Spanish and Japanese), the machines being hooked to brass stirrups.

All this signage equipment mediates between the vastness of the 'nave' and the very dense texture of the wall surfaces and dados of the rooms. The red lacquer and gleaming brass contrast with the matt quality of the brown concrete, the polished labels with the granular stone from Buxy which is used for the dados.

The graphics programme for the museum's visual identity is built upon three strong foundations: the typography, the logo and colour.

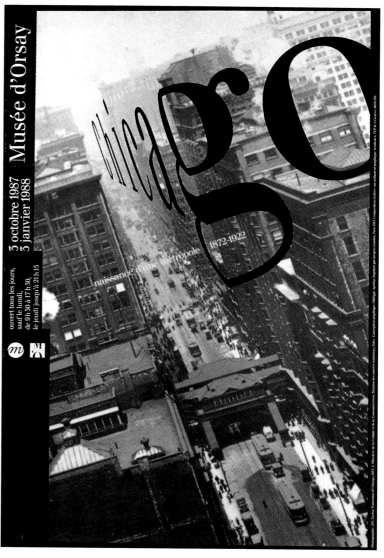

MUSEE D'ORSAY

Opposite: the brief guide provides visitors with basic information and a floor-plan. A brightly coloured flag makes it easy to identify at a glance the language of the leaflet, while the museum monogram is an unobtrusive pale grey.

Left and *above*: two posters by Philippe Apeloig achieve a good balance between original sepia photographs from the nineteenth century and computer lettering.

The basic element of the typography is Walbaum Buch, a typeface belonging to the Didot school, very similar in fact to Didot. Invented in the eighteenth century and widely used in the nineteenth century, the design of the letters combines grace, strength and severity, without creating any weakness in the serifs. At the time of the competition, Firmin Didot's original typeface had been proposed and selected, but it was later decided to use Walbaum Buch because of its more contemporary, present-day image.

It was while musing on the acronym 'MOMA' for the Museum of Modern Art, New York, that Monguzzi perfected the Musée d'Orsay's monogram: an 'M' above an 'O', separated by a fine line, like two exposures on a reel of film. It conveys a compact image and a suggestion of movement.

The use of colour falls into two categories: the monochrome range of white, black and grey represents the institutional image, while the sign system fulfilling a functional role employs white, black, grey, red, brown and green.

The graphics programme possesses great elegance, reflecting a harmonious alliance between the Swiss tradition and French culture. It has placed at the service of art a classic typography which truly 'serves' without competing. It is this that makes the programme historically significant.

Since the museum's opening, the competition graphics team retained an advisory role with a brief to maintain the consistency of the project.

MUSEE D'ORSAY

Samples from the original and harmonious interior sign system, which successfully mediates between the vastness of the nave (*right*) and the dense texture of the wall surfaces and dados of the rooms (*opposite, above*).

The exhibition label (*opposite, right*) can be slipped out of its brass frame and replaced, as required. The moveable brass horizontal bars indicate directions.

vers les expositions
du M'O

Dossier 5,
Photographie
et Arts
Graphiques 3

et le Restaurant

sortie

DEUTSCHES FILMMUSEUM

Previous page: the designers' diagrams reveal the steps from zoetrope to geometric symbol.

This page: the museum's identity for exhibitions (*below*) and for programmes for the municipal cinema (*above*) relies heavily on photographic images. *Above left*: the leaflet for the museum's opening.

A broadsheet on an exhibition of Wim Wenders' work.

Schauplätze
Kino–Reisen–Bilder
von Wim Wenders

" Ausstellung

" Wim Wenders

" Kino

" Reisen

" Bilder

" Musik

STADT FRANKFURT AM MAIN

deutsches filmmuseum frankfurt am main

Einladung

Einladung

Einladung

Einladung

DEUTSCHES FILMMUSEUM

A selection of printed material, all carrying the magic lantern symbol. *Above*: a series of invitations. *Left*: information leaflets for exhibitions. The range of colours used is sober: chiefly black, grey and white.

Opposite: two views of the museum's exhibition displays.

Science-Fiction-Film · Horrorfilm · Heimatfilm · Melodram · Abenteuerfilm · sical · Detektivfilm · Gangsterfilm · Western

Antinazi · B · Picture · Produzenten

Bayerisches Nationalmuseum
Munich

Designer **Mendell & Oberer: Pierre Mendell**
Work done **Posters, invitations, catalogues**
Year **1989**

The national museum of Bavaria was founded in 1855 by Maximilian II for the conservation of national treasures and other relics of the past. Since its first building was swiftly outgrown, it was decided in the 1890s to erect a new one on the Prinzregentenstrasse, which was opened in 1900. Gabriel Seidl's plans were among the most original of their day; the galleries were designed to suit their intended contents by varying their size, shape, decoration – even their floor level. Further extensions were made over the years, until in 1978 it was decided to embark on a full renovation (the building had been only partially repaired after serious damage in the Second World War).

The important treasures of the Wittelsbach royal family form the nucleus of the museum, but the variety of its collections is due to later acquisitions. Among the exhibits are rooms devoted to folk history, including a collection of nativity scenes; a historical survey from the early Middle Ages to the beginning of this century, with sculpture, paintings, furniture, tapestries and other craftwork; and specialist collections of ivories, clocks, porcelain, painted glass and miniatures.

Mendell's series of posters for the museum is part of a sustained policy of building an identity by the use of posters whose visual images are repeated on invitations and catalogues. This series derives its visual impact from a simple but original idea: focusing on a detail from a human figure and printing the museum name as if it were the label on an imaginary plinth. On each poster, the depiction of a single bust (from a painting, statue or reliquary) acts as a constant, but the angle of view, the colours and subject vary. The information is conveyed with the greatest expressiveness possible, without any superfluous frills. The basic rule for poster design, 'One idea, one message', underlies Mendell's creation. The graphics, with their refined, selective means of communication, endow the functional image with a significance that is undisguisedly related to sense as much as form. Like all Mendell & Oberer's designs, the method of expression is truly modern without blindly following fashion, combining originality, pragmatism and spirit.

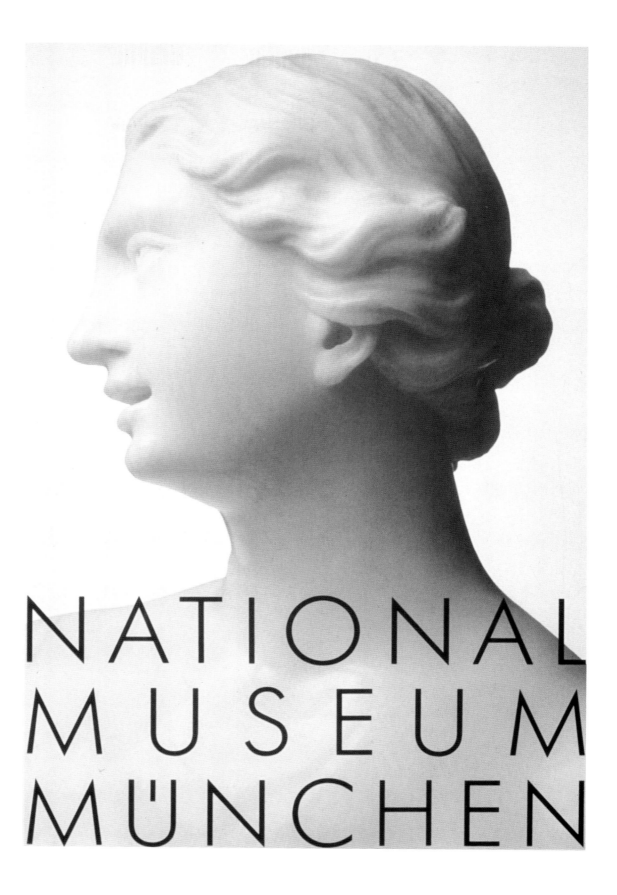

The museum's identity is established by a series of posters, each of which presents a striking visual image. These are repeated on invitations and catalogues. The regular collaboration between museum and designer has produced a refined, uncluttered functional image of considerable power.

NATIONAL MUSEUM MÜNCHEN

Die Neue Sammlung
Munich

Designer Mendell & Oberer: Pierre Mendell
Work done Posters, invitations, catalogues
Date 1984–1990

Die Neue Sammlung, Munich's museum of applied arts, has been housed in a sidewing of the Bayerisches Nationalmuseum since 1925. It can hold only temporary exhibitions, as there is insufficient room to show the permanent collection. The Bavarian state has, however, approved plans for two large new buildings: one in Nuremberg, scheduled for completion in 1995, and the other near the Alte Pinakothek in Munich, which should be ready in about 2000.

Pierre Mendell has been designing posters over a number of years for the museum. Examples illustrated here range from 1984 to 1990. A strong, continuous identity has been created from the posters by repeating the visuals on catalogues and invitations.

The visuals are always simple, so that the message can be swiftly assimilated. Different techniques for conveying it are brought into play from poster to poster, but the rapport between text and images is always excellent. The resulting graphic style is original and personal. It is characterized by the dynamism of the design, the leanness of the layout and the use of an enormously enlarged detail to catch the eye. All his designs capture the essential quality of their subject by the viewpoint selected, by focusing on a detail, and by the choice of the precisely appropriate text which creates a formal space of considerable beauty. The posters are all figurative, but the stylization of their subject is so great that they come close to abstraction. The designer's inventiveness takes them beyond merely fulfilling a utilitarian role and endows them with a lasting appeal.

Armin Hofmann
Graphic Design
Die Neue Sammlung
Di–So 10–17 Uhr
27.10.89–
14.1.90

Mendell & Oberer's posters for Die Neue Sammlung share certain characteristics: dynamic designs; spare, uncluttered layouts; and a tendency to focus on an enlarged detail (such as wheels to represent cars).

Left: monochrome poster for an exhibition of the graphic design work of Armin Hofmann (1989). *Opposite, above*: posters explaining that the museum is closed for building works (1984) and publicizing an exhibition on designing cars (1986). *Below*: posters for an exhibition of Japanese posters (1989) and an exhibition of posters designed by painters, such as Miró and Picasso, mainly for their own work.

Geschlossen!

Aufgrund von Umbauten des Gebäudes fallen die Ausstellungen der Neuen Sammlung für mehrere Monate aus. Die Museumsarbeit wird jedoch fortgesetzt.

Die Neue Sammlung Staatliches Museum für angewandte Kunst Prinzregentenstraße 3 8000 München 22

Ceterum censeo, hoc museum esse amplificandum.

Design
Process
Auto

22.11.86 –
8.2.87

Japanische Plakate 1960 bis heute

26. Oktober 1988
bis 15. Januar 1989
Dienstag bis Sonntag
10 bis 17 Uhr
Die Neue Sammlung
Prinzregentenstrasse 3
München

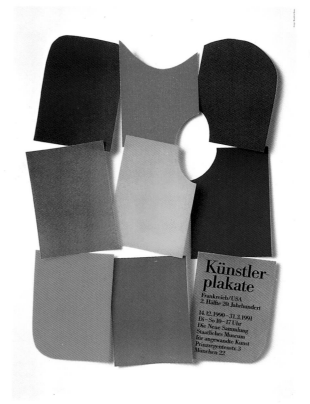

Künstler-
plakate

Frankreich/USA
2. Hälfte 20. Jahrhundert

14.12.1990–31.3.1991
Di–So 10–17 Uhr
Die Neue Sammlung
Staatliches Museum
für angewandte Kunst
Prinzregentenstr. 3
München 22

Werkstatt Berlin
Berlin

Designer Hard Werken Design: Gerard Hadders (design and art direction) Laura Genninger (typographic layout)
Work done Programme
Year 1988

The development of the arts today is characterized by the removal of traditional barriers between the cultural forms, disciplines and genres. The aim of Werkstatt was to further this by inviting artists from different countries to work in cooperation with each other, to integrate different fields and to develop new concepts. Areas represented included music, dance, theatre, fashion, design and the fine arts. Young artists and people interested in the arts were able to participate actively through classes, seminars and numerous workshops, as well as sitting in on working sessions. The one-off event was funded by the municipality of Berlin as part of the city's year as cultural capital of Europe.

The programme was designed by Hard Werken, a poster occupying one side and details about events the other. The poster visual is an interpretation of Berlin's traditional bear symbol, formed by combining positive and negative cut-outs of lead and copper. The bear, its jaws wide open, immediately has the maximum impact. The typography is treated as an ornamental device. Each unit of information is printed against a white background that looks like a cut-out raised above the surface. The edges of the cut-outs follow, with embellishments, the shape made by the typeset lines. Each heading – fine arts, dance, music, theatre, and so on – is computer set in different ways, while the more detailed information is set in classic typography (photocomposition). This is made even easier to read by ranging left the lines within the cut-outs.

On the reverse of the poster, the visual image of the bear is picked up, but cropped differently, and the computer word-images are repeated as the section headings. The text is set in small blocks. It is made easier to differentiate between information in German and English by centring lines in German but justifying those in English, while information on time and place is made more conspicuous by ranging it left.

The originality of the concept and the impact made by the composition of the whole turn as much on meaning as on form, expressed in an original language that beguiles the reader into the artist's esoteric world.

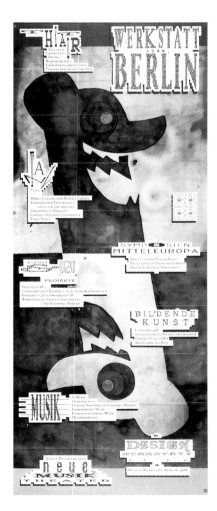

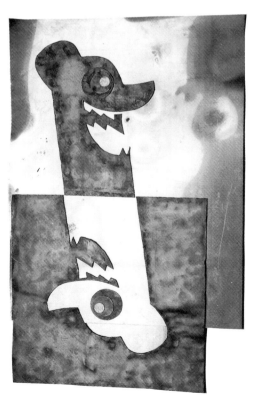

Hard Werken came up with an interpretation of Berlin's traditional bear symbol for their poster-cum-programme for the Werkstatt held in 1988. The poster image (*far left*) was produced by combining positive and negative cut-outs of lead and copper (*left*).

Poster dimensions: *c.* 16½ × 41 in (42 × 105 cm); *c.* 4 × 8 in (10½ × 21 cm) folded.

The Deutsches Architekturmuseum, which is housed in a renovated building on the Schaumainkai, was founded in 1979 by Heinrich Klotz. The emphasis is placed principally, but not exclusively, on 20th-century German architecture. Its permanent collection has been structured as a comparative selection of international projects and it is intended that the archive should eventually contain at least one project of every important 20th-century architect, from the first sketch to the final version. In addition to its permanent collection, temporary exhibitions, both historical and monographic, are mounted. Because of restricted space, large events are held elsewhere in a specially designed hall shared with other Frankfurt institutions. The museum publishes not only catalogues of its exhibitions, but also a quarterly journal and books on German architectural history and theory. Public discussions, conferences and symposia are regularly organized. In all this vigorous programme of activities, the single criterion for inclusion is quality.

Illner and Teufel's logo is made up of an original drawing of the museum's three initials (DAM), each letter being enclosed within a square. These drawings may be printed in either positive or negative, and appear on all museum documents, whether administrative or intended for the public. The vertically elongated information leaflets are enlivened by primary colours, used in highly architectural compositions. Photographs are sometimes introduced but are

Deutsches Architekturmuseum
Frankfurt am Main

Designer Projekt Design: Günter Illner, Philipp Teufel
Work done Logo, leaflets, stationery
Year 1985 onwards

handled graphically: the use of daylight printing, coarse-grain line subjects, cut-outs, and so on. The overall aesthetics reflect contemporary architecture and its visual representation. Posters, leaflets, invitations, all keep to certain typographic rules and fixed guidelines for the positioning of visuals. It is in fact the attention paid to applying the identity's typographic rules that produces its homogeneity and gives meaning to the graphics. The refinement of form and contents and the quality of its typography are what distinguish this identity so clearly from others.

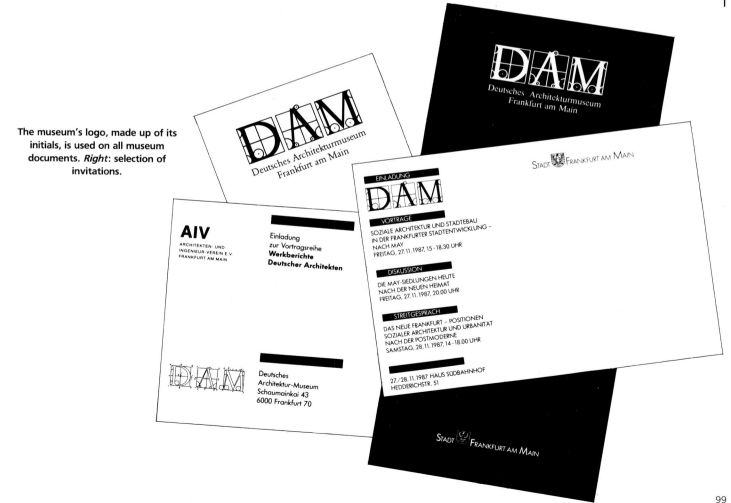

The museum's logo, made up of its initials, is used on all museum documents. *Right*: selection of invitations.

Aus Anlaß des 100. Geburtstages von Ernst May zeigt die Ausstellung erstmalig einen Großteil der Originalpläne und bindet sie in die zeitgenössische sozialpolitische Konstellation ein. Neue und historische Architekturfotografien der Frankfurter Siedlungen sowie Einzelbauten bedeutender Mitarbeiter Ernst Mays wie Martin Elsaesser oder Adolf Meyer komplettieren die Bestandsaufnahme des „Neuen Frankfurt". Zentrum der Ausstellung ist ein begehbares Wohnungsmodell mit Original-Mobiliar. Zur Ausstellung erscheint ein Katalog.

13. Dezember 1986 bis 15. Februar 1987

Die Ausstellung zeigt Modelle, Zeichnungen und Möbel von Mies van der Rohe, seinen Mitarbeitern wie K. L. Hilberseimer und seinen Schülern. Die Exponate wurden vom Art Institute in Chicago mit Unterstützung der Paul and Gabriella Rosenbaum Foundation zusammengetragen und werden durch Leihgaben aus der Bundesrepublik ergänzt.

Zur Ausstellung erscheint die deutsche Ausgabe des Kataloges.

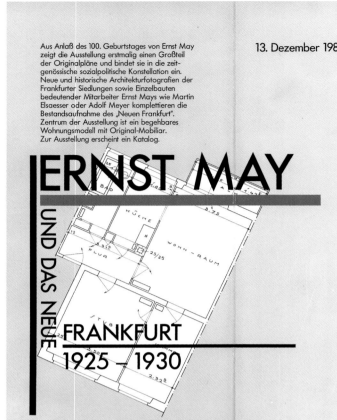

ERNST MAY
UND DAS NEUE FRANKFURT
1925 – 1930

MIES VAN DER ROHE
VORBILD UND VERMÄCHTNIS

ZURÜCK IN DIE ZUKUNFT SOZIALER ARCHITEKTUR

27./28.11.1987 HAUS SÜDBAHNHOF HEDDERICHSTR. 51

ERNST MAY KOLLOQUIUM

DEUTSCHES ARCHITEKTURMUSEUM FRANKFURT AM MAIN

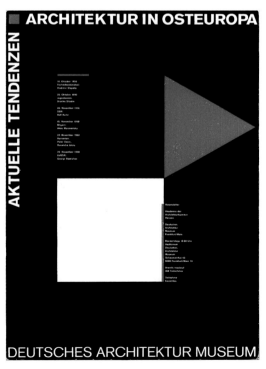

ARCHITEKTUR IN OSTEUROPA

AKTUELLE TENDENZEN

DEUTSCHES ARCHITEKTUR MUSEUM

CHERNIKHOV
ARCHITEKTONISCHE
FANTASIEN

Einladung

Zur Eröffnung der Ausstellung

**CHERNIKHOV
ARCHITEKTONISCHE
FANTASIEN**

Dienstag, den 15. August 1989,
17.00 Uhr im Schaudepot des
Deutschen Architekturmuseums.

Pressevorbesichtigung:
15. August, 15.00 Uhr
Pressekonferenz: 16.00 Uhr

Zur Eröffnung der Ausstellung
spricht:
Andrei Chernikhov

Hilmar Hoffmann
Dezernent
für Kultur und Freizeit

Leiter des
Deutschen Architekturmuseums

Dauer der Ausstellung:
16.08.–20.09.1989

Öffnungszeiten:
Di.–So. 10.00–17.00 Uhr,
Mi. 10.00–20.00 Uhr,
Mo. geschlossen

Zur Ausstellung erscheint
ein Katalog

Die Ausstellung entstand in
Zusammenarbeit mit der
Deutschen Lufthansa AG
und dem International Forum
of Young Architects

⊛ **Lufthansa**

DEUTSCHES ARCHITEKTURMUSEUM

The identity's homogeneity derives from the use of strong grids, from
its adherence to its typographic rules and from the application of fixed
guidelines to the positioning of visual images.

**Vortragsreihe
1991**

Werkberichte Deutscher Architekten

Januar	**Jakubeit**		
	Barbara Jakubeit, Präsidentin der Bundesbaudirektion, Bonn	19.00 Uhr Auditorium des Deutschen Architektur-Museums	15.01.1991
Januar	**van den Valentyn**		
	Thomas van den Valentyn, Büro van den Valentyn, Köln	19.00 Uhr Auditorium des Deutschen Architektur-Museums	29.01.1991
Februar	**Natterer**		
	Julius Natterer (EPFL Lausanne), Büro Natterer, CH – Etoy	19.00 Uhr Auditorium des Deutschen Architektur-Museums	19.02.1991

**Vortragsreihe
1990**

Werkberichte Deutscher Architekten

November	**Eisele, Fritz**		
	Jo Eisele (TH Darmstadt), Nico Fritz, Büro Eisele & Fritz, Darmstadt	19.00 Uhr Auditorium des Deutschen Architektur-Museums	06.11.1990
November	**Herzog**		
	Thomas Herzog (TH Darmstadt), Büro Thomas Herzog, München / Darmstadt	19.00 Uhr Auditorium des Deutschen Architektur-Museums	20.11.1990
Dezember	**Ganz, Rolfes**		
	Joachim Ganz, Walter Rolfes, Büro Ganz und Rolfes, Berlin	19.00 Uhr Auditorium des Deutschen Architektur-Museums	04.12.1990
Dezember	**Kuhler**		
	Ingeborg Kuhler (HdK Berlin), Büro Prof. Kuhler, Mannheim	19.00 Uhr Auditorium des Deutschen Architektur-Museums	18.12.1990

MUSEUMS ARCHITEKTUR IN FRANKFURT
1980 1990

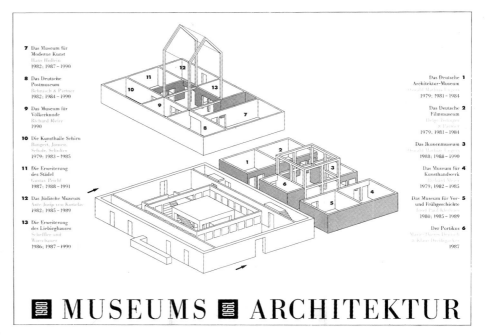

7 Das Museum für
Moderne Kunst
Hans Hollein
1982; 1987–1990

8 Das Deutsche
Postmuseum
Behnisch & Partner
1982; 1984–1990

9 Das Museum für
Völkerkunde
Richard Meier
1990

10 Die Kunsthalle Schirn
Bangert, Jansen,
Scholz, Schultes
1979; 1983–1985

11 Die Erweiterung
des Städel
Gustav Peichl
1987; 1988–1991

12 Das Jüdische Museum
Ante Josip von Kostelac
1982; 1985–1988

13 Die Erweiterung
des Liebieghauses
Scheffler und
Warschauer
1986; 1987–1990

Das Deutsche 1
Architektur-Museum
Oswald Mathias Ungers
1979; 1981–1984

Das Deutsche 2
Filmmuseum
Helge Bofinger
& Partner
1979; 1981–1984

Das Ikonenmuseum 3
Oswald Mathias Ungers
1988; 1988–1990

Das Museum für 4
Kunsthandwerk
Richard Meier
1979; 1982–1985

Das Museum für Vor- 5
und Frühgeschichte
Josef Paul Kleihues
1980; 1985–1989

Der Portikus 6
Marie-Theres Deutsch
& Klaus Dreissigacker
1987

1980 MUSEUMS 1990 ARCHITEKTUR

DÄM
Deutsches Architekturmuseum
Frankfurt am Main

JÜDISCHES MUSEUM

DIE ARCHITEKTUR DER SYNAGOGE

In der Nacht vom 9. auf den 10. November 1938
brannten in ganz Deutschland die Synagogen,
jüdische Geschäfte wurden zerstört, fast 100 Men-
schen bestialisch ermordet, zehntausende in die
Konzentrationslager verschleppt: der größte Pogrom
der Neuzeit und doch nur ein Auftakt für den mit
der technokratischen Akribie deutscher Beamten-
tums durchgeführten Holocaust.

Eine Ausstellung, die 50 Jahre nach diesen Verbre-
chen aufzeigen soll, welch ein wichtiger Bereich aus
der Architektur seit jener Zeit aus unserer städtischen
Umwelt verschwunden ist und versuchen will, der
„Architektur der Synagoge" den ihr gebührenden
Platz in der Architekturgeschichte zurückzugeben,
wäre ohne die Erinnerung an die Schrecken der in
naß-forschem Zynismus als „Reichskristallnacht"
bezeichneten Pogrome nicht vollständig.

Dennoch sollen die Pläne und Zeichnungen, die
Gemälde und Architekturfragmente, die Modelle
und Rekonstruktionen vor allem den Reichtum die-
ser in der Architekturgeschichtsschreibung noch
immer arg vernachlässigten Bautradition sinnfällig
vor Augen führen – einer Tradition, die seit dem
3. Jahrhundert v. u. Z. besteht – wenn sie auch immer
wieder durch Verfolgungen und Vertreibungen unter-
brochen wurde.

Im Gegensatz zu Kirche und Tempel ist die Synagoge
(hebr.: Beth Haknesset = Versammlungshaus) nie
ein durch Opfer und postulierte göttliche Anwesen-
heit geheiligter Ort gewesen, sondern ein Mehr-
zweckbau, Stätte der Versammlung, des Gebets und
der Lehre. Spezielle architektonische Würdeformen
brauchten für einen derartigen Nutzbau also nicht
entwickelt zu werden. Später kam noch hinzu, daß
die jüdischen Gemeinden in der Diaspora versuchen
mußten, sich ihrer jeweiligen Umgebung bis zur
Assimilation anzupassen.

Zahlreiche baupolizeiliche Vorschriften und die
Konkurrenz der christlichen Kirchen engten die
architektonischen Möglichkeiten weiter ein.

Andererseits spiegeln gerade deswegen die überlie-
ferten Bauwerke in ganz besonderer Weise die politi-
schen, kulturellen und sozialen Verhältnisse wieder,
unter denen sie entstanden und legen darüber
hinaus Zeugnis ab für den kulturellen Reichtum,
der in jenem gesellschaftlichen Spannungsfeld ent-
stehen konnte, in dem sich die jüdischen Gemeinden
in der Diaspora einzurichten hatten. Es dürfte kaum
einen zweiten Bautypus in der Architekturgeschichte
geben, bei dem Stil- und Gesellschaftsgeschichte so
unmittelbar miteinander korrespondieren wie bei der
Synagoge.

Fußbodenmosaik, Synagoge Beth Shean 6. Jh. u. u. Z.

Synagoge Horb, Decken- und Wandmalereien, 18. Jh.

Max Beckmann, Synagoge, 1919.

DEUTSCHES ARCHITEKTURMUSEUM

Leaflets for an exhibition on museum architecture in Frankfurt (*opposite, above*) and for a joint project with the Jüdisches Museum on the architecture of synagogues (*below*).

Right: exhibition poster.

DEUTSCHES ARCHITEKTURMUSEUM FRANKFURT AM MAIN · SCHAUMAINKAI 43

FRANKFURT PROJEKT

CHRISTOPH MÄCKLER

17.1. – 15. 2.1987 · DI. BIS SO.10 – 17 UHR · MI.10 – 20 UHR · MO. GESCHLOSSEN

STADT FRANKFURT AM MAIN

Kiel Week
Kiel

Designers Jean Widmer, Visuel Design (1980). Bruno K. Wiese, Visual Design (1982). Ernst Hiestand (1984). Rudi Meyer (1987). Nicolas Girard, Zéro 2 (1989). Ben Bos, Total Design (1991)
Work done Posters, programmes, banners, promotional material
Year Various

Kiel Week, an international sailing and cultural festival, traces its origins back more than a hundred years to 1882, when it was founded by yachtsmen as a racing regatta. Its scope has been broadened considerably since 1948 to include other activities, with the permanent objective of contributing to world peace and fostering international understanding. Since then, the town council has organized an annual competition open to European graphic designers. The winner is chosen from among seven contestants to develop the entire visual identity of the festival for that year.

Each year a different theme is selected, around which a wide range of activities is organized. The nine-day 'Week' is packed full of things to do, open to visitors of all ages and from all countries: concerts, both jazz and classical; discos; dances; acrobatic displays; regattas; readings by authors; theatre; art exhibitions.

The designers take up the annual theme, expressed in a short slogan, and reinforce it by means of their graphic response. The list of themes and winning designers is too long to comment on each individually, but the following is a selection from recent years.

1991 'A technological future – nightmare or ray of hope?': white sails plough a white wake across a deep blue sea against a turquoise sky (Ben Bos, Amsterdam).

1990 'Town and Nature': an evocation of yacht sails in solid colours (Rosmarie Tissi, Zurich).

1989 'Living and working – the chances in the North': typographic layout of the dates and title in a Constructivist style (Nicolas Girard, Paris).

1988 'Media – power – opinions': primary colours printed solid, on a white background, with vertical text (Ahmad Moualla, Paris).

1987 'Under full sail': white slashes on a dark-blue background are especially evocative of the lightness of yacht sails (Rudi Meyer, Paris).

1986 'Health – everyone's business': white window on blue. Simple, elegant typography (Ruedi Baur, Lyon).

Six decades of Kiel Week from 1948, when the event took on its current form. Designers: Niels Brodersen, Kiel (1948); G. W. Hörnig, Hamburg (1952); Bernard Borgwardt, Kiel (1955); Walter Breker, Düsseldorf (1960); F. K. Boes, Düsseldorf (1967); Hans Förtsch, Berlin (1976).

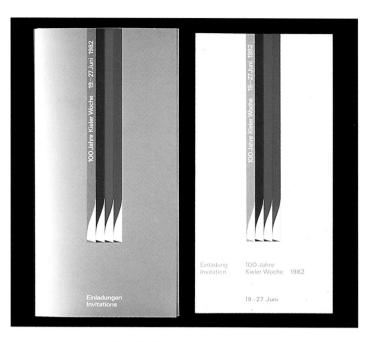

Jean Widmer's graphics for 1980 (*below*) and Bruno K. Wiese's 1982 design both place emphasis on the vertical, an approach inspired by yacht sails. 1982 was the event's centenary year.

1984 'Peace: living in – keeping up – working for': geometric forms in primary colours on a blue background (Ernst Hiestand, Zurich).

1982 'Art in our town': sails in violet, blue and green, or shades of red. The silver background gives emphasis to the vertical white typography (Bruno K. Wiese, Hamburg).

1980 'Sport: games, performance and risk': large black and white photographs. The shape of the leaflet echoes the graphics inspired by the yachts (Jean Widmer, Paris).

The applications of the logo have varied from year to year: posters and brochures; plaques to be affixed to yachts; stickers; hats, scarves and ties; street signs and Morris columns.

In spite of the variety of themes, the dominant graphic interpretation is stylized, spread sails, used to varying decorative effects. The international juries have been rigorous in their adjudication and have pursued a coherent graphics style, inspired by the Swiss school, from year to year.

KIEL WEEK

Below and left: **Ernst Hiestand's geometric design (1984).**
Opposite left: **merchandise, programmes and poster by Rudi Meyer (1987).** *Opposite, right*: **Nicolas Girard's design for 1989.**

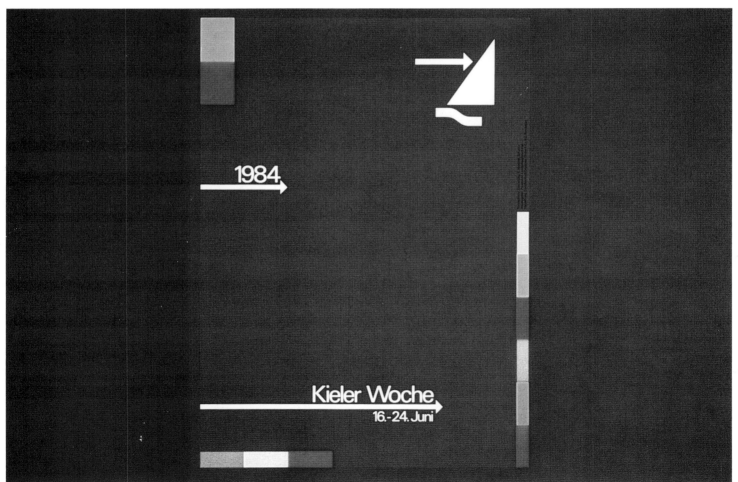

1984

Kieler Woche
16.-24. Juni

Kieler Woche 1987

20.–
28. Juni

design Rudi Meyer, Paris

Juni 16.–25.
Kieleri
Woche
1988

Programm
Offizielles
Programmheft
der Landeshauptstadt Kiel

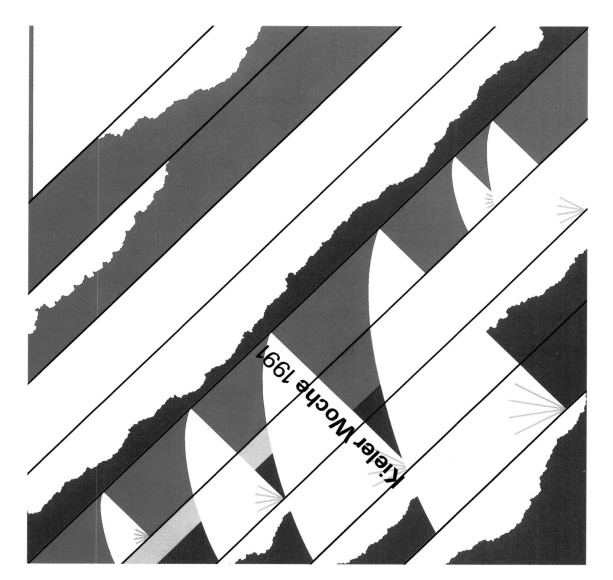

Kieler Woche 1991

Kieler Woche
22.-30. Juni 1991

Kieler Woche
22.-30. Juni 1991

Kieler Woche
22.-30. Juni 1991

Kieler Woche
22.-30. Juni 1991

KIEL WEEK

Ben Bos's (Total Design) winning entry for 1991 is an interpretation of wind-filled sails. Its dynamic springs from the horizontal or oblique lines. The design follows the Kiel tradition of stylization almost to the point of abstraction.

Kieler Woche

22.-30. Juni 1991

ITALY

Castello di Rivoli
Rivoli

Designers **Armando Testa. Extra Studio: Armando Ceste**
Work done **Trademark and logo (Testa); invitations, press kits,
brochure (Ceste)**
Year **1986**

The museum of contemporary art housed in the Castello di Rivoli was founded in 1984 on the initiative of the region of Piedmont. It owes its existence to the efforts of voluntary societies, who have succeeded in making it in recent years an important point of reference in the arts world.

The building dates from the fourteenth century and was renovated between 1979 and 1984 by the architect Andrea Bruno. He designed elements that can be dismantled – balconies, windows, suspended staircases – so that the spaces can be used in different ways and then returned to their original form.

For the museum's opening exhibition, many artists, including Sol Lewitt and Mario Merz, were invited to create a work for a specific setting in the museum. The castle has been transformed into an exhibition gallery which houses a permanent collection of works by living artists. The final stage of the building programme provided it with a library, restaurant and information centre.

The museum graphics are very simple: a logo consisting of a classical architectural element – an arch – accompanied by Univers typography, all in capitals. The range of colours includes red, blue and gold, printed solid, usually on a granular, matt paper. The museum's stationery is printed in black on white paper.

The graphic design and publishing plan for the Castello di Rivoli were devised and executed in cooperation with Rudi Fuchs and Johannes Gachnang (museum directors) and Cristina Mundici.

**A selection of the Castello's
stationery, printed in black
on white paper.**

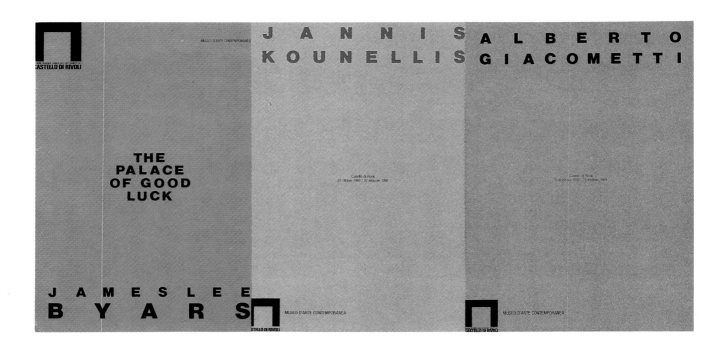

CASTELLO DI RIVOLI

Opposite : publicity folders and invitations to private views for a variety of temporary exhibitions. The colours change, but the black logo remains constant.

Below : part of the long, wrap-around cover from the spiral-bound brochure which introduces the museum. The illusionist pattern is executed in shades of grey and stone. *Right* : the museum's architectural logo (detail from the cover below).

Venti progetti per il futuro del Lingotto

Turin

Designer Gregotti Associati: Pierluigi Cerri
Work done Visuals, exterior sign
Year 1983–84

In 1982, after sixty years as a major car plant, Lingotto ceased production. When it was opened in Turin in 1920, it was a landmark in industrial history; its sheer size, vertical structure and famous roof-top test track were all symbols of technological progress. Many of Fiat's best-known models were designed and manufactured there. When production ended, Fiat searched for new uses for the enormous area. As part of this process, they invited twenty architects from all over the world to submit their proposals; the result was *Venti progetti per il futuro del Lingotto* ('Twenty projects for Lingotto's future'). The only condition was that their plans should respect the characteristics of the original plant.

As a result of the debate sparked off by their submissions, it was decided to convert Lingotto to a multi-purpose centre dedicated to innovation that would bring together producers and users of advanced technology. The designs were by Renzo Piano.

Pierluigi Cerri was responsible for the visuals and sign system of the exhibition of the twenty proposals put forward. The graphic image consisted of a group of sculptural letters of the alphabet set up outside the factory, which together spelled out 'Lingotto'. The three-dimensional letters, which stood directly on the ground, were enormous, rising about 12 feet (4 metres) into the air. A particular rhythm was imparted to the group as a whole by their different orientations, some upright, some at an angle. The colours – a range of blues, greens, red and yellow – achieved an especial vibrancy because of the industrial architecture that formed the backdrop.

The three-dimensional letters spelling out 'Lingotto' formed the exterior sign for the exhibition to decide the future of the Lingotto factory. They were large enough to dwarf people walking through them – and to avoid being dwarfed by the majestic Lingotto building. Their bright colours provided a dramatic contrast to the surrounding grey steel architecture.

Museo Poldi Pezzoli
Milan

Designer Italo Lupi
Work done Logo, stationery, interior sign system
Year 1988

The Museo Poldi Pezzoli offers valuable evidence for private collecting trends in the nineteenth century and aims to achieve a harmonious unity of works of art, furniture and atmosphere. The collection belonged to Gian Giacomo Poldi Pezzoli, who in 1850 began to extend it to include not just arms and armour, but a wide variety of art forms: paintings, sculpture, carpets, tapestries, ceramics, glass, archaeological finds, jewellery, furniture and so on. As the result of Poldi Pezzoli's generous legacy, the collection was opened to the public in 1881. In the twentieth century, the museum was rebuilt after being bombed in 1943 and was reopened in 1951. Since then, it has extended its collections to include, for instance, a large collection of mechanical clocks, and

also sundials. Among the artists ranging from the fourteenth to the nineteenth centuries whose paintings are now on show are Pollaiuolo, Botticelli, Piero della Francesca, Mantegna, Luini, Guardi, Canaletto and Tiepolo.

The simple components of the visual identity were invented by Lupi to create an atmosphere which evokes the museum's historical collections, its refinement and age. The composition of the logo, consisting of three graphic signs – the letter 'M' and two profiles like those on Italian Renaissance cameos, produces a calm image reminiscent of painting. Lupi successfully combines a visual identity treated in a contemporary manner with a representation of the fascinating legacy of the museum's collections. Without stooping to mere imitation or adopting a servile attitude towards the works of art on show, the graphics come up to the level set by the distinguished paintings. The use of a fine-ruled line, of empty and full space, of symmetrical placing, all serve to treat the printing of the museum name as a formal object. The layout of the printed word shows good judgment. Without overt inducement, it generates enough curiosity to make the viewer want to know the museum better. The banners for outside the building reproduce the same elements in soft tones of blue, pinks and lilac.

The museum logo (*left*) is a mixture of typography and pictorial image in black on white. The profiles recall cameos of the Italian Renaissance, but they also echo the 'Ps' of the museum's name. Banners to hang outside the building (*below*) use the same elements on soft backgrounds of blue, lilac-grey, coral and pink.

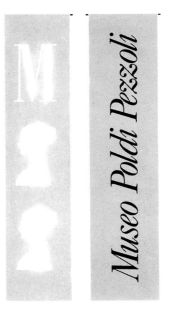

The Palazzo Grassi, whose façade overlooks the Grand Canal, was designed (*c.* 1740) by the important Venetian architect, Giorgio Massari. In 1984, it was bought by Fiat to provide a centre for the promotion of both the arts and sciences, past and present. The architects Gae Aulenti and Antonio Foscari were commissioned to restore the building (1985–86), with a brief to stay true to the spirit of the 18th-century architecture.

In 1984, soon after Fiat's purchase of the palace, the Palazzo Grassi corporation was founded, its objective being to highlight the interaction between art and science through exhibitions and associated activities. Equal importance was attached to encouraging a critical reexamination of the past by organizing historical exhibitions to shed light on the evolution of culture and technology. It was in pursuit of this ideal that Fiat chose as the theme of the Palazzo's opening exhibition *Futurismo e Futurismi* (1986).

The Palazzo's institutional image rests upon a typographical logo, in both a positive (black on white) and negative version, which was designed by Pierluigi Cerri (1984–85). The manner in which the typography is used, with the letters pressed very close together, or even interlinked, is more important than the actual choice of typeface. This graphic image suits the coherence of the architecture and reflects supremely well the Palazzo's combination of past and present. Possessing considerable subtlety, the unmistakable logo achieves

Palazzo Grassi
Venice

Designer Gregotti Associati: Pierluigi Cerri
Work done Logo, promotional material
Year 1984–85, 1986, 1987

instant recognition when seen on all the documents intended for the public.

The Palazzo does not, however, communicate through a monolithic identity. For each event, a visual image is designed to pick up the feel of the work of the artist who is the subject of the show. The resulting graphics do not fall into the trap of mimicry, but succeed in living up to standards set by their artist-subjects. The images produced are clean, clear, strong, and possess perfect layouts. Their quality is so exceptional that nothing else is needed to support them. The emphasis is placed more on the separate events than on the institutional aspect of the centre.

The Palazzo's typographic logo creates an intriguing pattern by the way in which the letters are pressed closely together, or even interlinked.

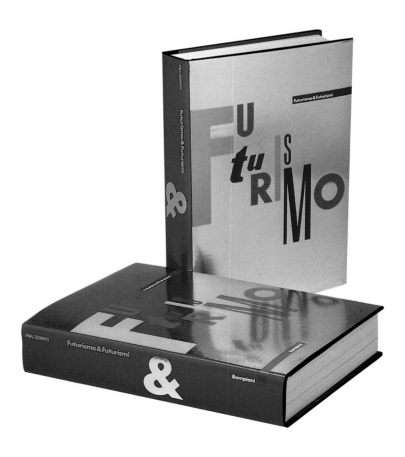

The Palazzo does not operate a monolithic identity. A different visual image is created for each exhibition, which might not include the institution's logo.

Right and *opposite, below*: poster and catalogue for the Palazzo's opening exhibition. *Opposite, above* and *left*: logo and bag for the 1987 Tinguely exhibition.

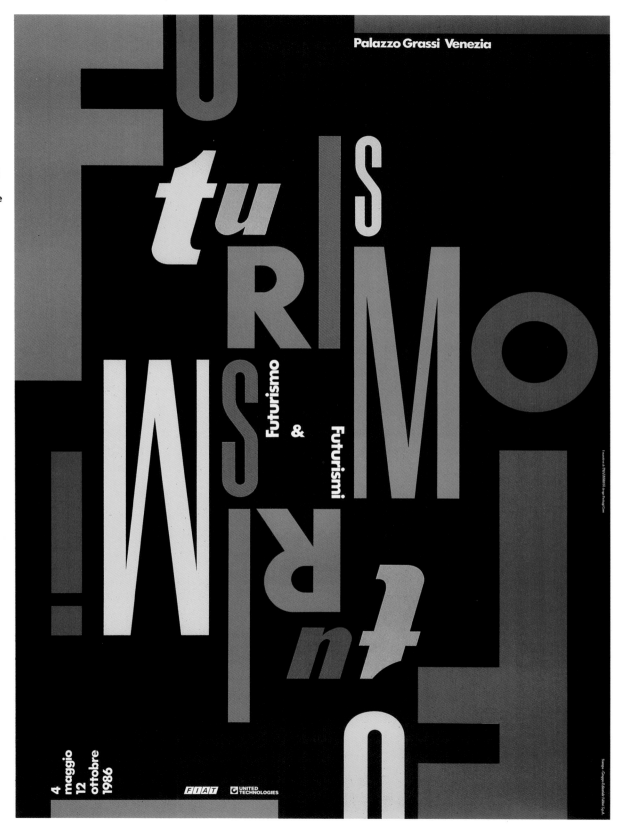

Palazzo Grassi Venezia

Futurismo & Futurismi

4 maggio 12 ottobre 1986

F/I/A/T   UNITED TECHNOLOGIES

Venice Biennale
Venice

Designer **Tapiro**
Work done **Posters, invitations**
Year **1985**

The Venice Biennale, founded in 1895, takes place mainly in the autumn. International in scope, it brings together multidisciplinary events such as cinema, theatre, sculpture, photography, and so on, from all over the world. The works for exhibition are selected by panels of experts, which change every two years. The events, which are organized by theme (painting, music, cinema, etc.), take place in different locations. In addition, countries have their own national pavilions.

For the Biennale's ninetieth anniversary, the visual identity of all the events was based on a reinterpretation, in a contemporary script, of the festival's first symbol, designed by Augusto Sézanne in 1895. The various events each had

their own different printed material – invitations, posters and so on. Their identity was established graphically by the use of their own different frameworks. These nevertheless kept to the typography of the overall identity. This acted as a visual unifier, superimposed on the distinctive graphic symbols for the various events. The illustrations representing the different aspects of the festival were of psychedelic inspiration, executed in pastel colours which enhance the subtle layouts.

Below: the poster to celebrate the Biennale's ninetieth anniversary incorporates the original 1895 poster. *Below left*: catalogue to accompany the international art show of June 1986.

Milan Triennale
Milan

Designer Italo Lupi
Work done Visual image, posters, catalogue covers
Year 1983–86

Since 1923, the Milan Triennale has organized international expositions. Their theme has always been the world of design projects and the world of the city, both architecturally and in the design of everyday objects, whether produced industrially or by artisans. The festival's activities are always characterized by a desire to select the most innovative tendencies and to promote debate aimed at producing a collective leap forward in taste.

The festival began life as a Biennale of the Decorative Arts at Monza. Since 1933, however, the Triennale has had its seat in the Palazzo dell'Arte in the Parco Sempione, Milan. Designed by the architect Giovanni Muzio to provide a flexible setting for the Triennale, the Palazzo underwent a radical restoration from 1979 to 1984. Bare of ornamentation, the building remains one of the best exhibition venues because of the rich variety of the use of space during the festival.

Italo Lupi designed posters and related catalogues for several exhibitions of the XVIIth Triennale. The two selected here are 'Le case della Triennale' (1983) and 'Il progetto domestico' (1986). The illustrations for each are very different in technique, and make a harmonious game of the connection between graphics and typography.

For 'Le case della Triennale', stencil-style lettering was used to make up the exhibition's name. The letters are formed from geometric shapes drawn in pastel, complemented by geometric blocks in bold black. The typography of the title actually becomes the image of the poster and catalogue, rather like an architect's title stamp.

For 'Il progetto domestico', Lupi employs the graphic language of architects: drawing, outline perspective, noting the dimensions of spaces, black outlines as if using drawing-pens, solid colours, and so on.

The graphics policy of the Triennale is affirmed by the range of commissions awarded to graphic artists, without any concern for achieving coherence from one event to another.

Left: the poster for 'Il progetto domestico' portrays a house interior in the graphic language of architects (colours: white, bright yellow, red).
Below: catalogue cover with stencil-style lettering in red, gold, blue, brown and green on white.

JAPAN

Watari-Um
Tokyo

Designer Space 606: Ryoichi Kondo. Eye-Some Design Inc.:
Chihiro Shigeyama. Katsumi Asaba
Work done Logo, stationery, publications, merchandise
Year 1990

Watari-Um, or the Watari Museum of Contemporary Art, is a small private museum which was opened in Tokyo in September 1990. It hosts exhibitions of contemporary art and architecture, as well as films, live performances and lectures. Artists represented include Joseph Beuys and Gilbert and George.

In 1985 the Swiss architect Mario Botta was commissioned by Shizuko Watari to design a museum building for the site on which the Galerie Watari originally stood. The brief presented two particular problems. What had once been a rectangular plot of land had been turned into a small triangular plot by the building of a new road. In addition, Tokyo imposes stringent building requirements because of its experiences with earthquakes and fire. Botta fitted into the space a six-storey building – his first museum – based on the triangle, and ingeniously arranged inside to appear bigger than it really is. Three storeys serve as exhibition floors; there is a bookshop in the basement, a museum shop on the ground floor. The Western nature of the art on show is counterbalanced by a room designed for the Japanese tea ceremony. Materials for the interior vary; brick walls painted white with a white floor; cloth-covered walls with a slate floor. The exterior is visually striking: rough white concrete divided into bands by rows of grey natural stones. In Botta's words, 'The whole façade resembles a bird spreading its wings and stretches out along the road as far as possible in order to make best use of the lot.'

The building's striking elevation directly inspired the logo created by graphic designer Ryoichi Kondo, which reproduces in monochrome the façade with its decorative horizontal banding.

The colour scheme for museum stationery and publications reflects the architecture: black, grey, white, sometimes silver. The text and headings are usually bilingual, in English and Japanese. The typography is straightforward. Colours are printed solid, on good-quality paper. For each exhibition, a key colour is chosen that appears on associated material, and is also used for the title of the newsletter covering the relevant period.

Cover of the bilingual catalogue (designed by Chihiro Shigeyama) to accompany the museum's opening exhibition explaining the history of Mario Botta's design for the building. The photograph shows a detail of the museum's principal façade and emphasizes the decorative effect of the natural stone and concrete banding. It was the linear pattern of the façade that inspired the museum's symbol (see overleaf): the building is the linchpin of the institution's visual identity.

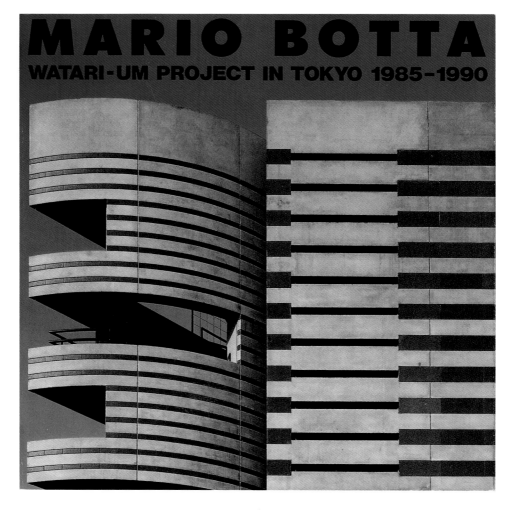

123

WATARI-UM
The Watari Museum of Contemporary Art

WATARI-UM
The Watari Museum of Contemporary Art
News Letter

March April May 1991
Vol 3

渋谷局

料金別納
郵便

WATARI-UM
The Watari Museum of Contemporary Art

3-7-6 Jingumae Shibuya-ku
Tokyo 150 Japan
Tel.03/3402-3001 Fax.03/3478-0809

WATARI-UM
The Watari Musenm of Contemporary Art

3-7-6 Jinguma
Tokyo 15
Tel.03/3402-3001 F

WATARI-UM
The Watari Museum of Contemporary Art

3-7-6 Jingumae Shibuya-ku
Tokyo 150 Japan
Tel.03/3402-3001 Fax.03/3478-0809

Shizuko Watari

WATARI-UM

The logo (*opposite, top*) consists of a diagram of Botta's façade. It has two forms: positive, in which the pale concrete is represented by white, reversed out within a black circle or set against a black background; and negative, in which the concrete is represented by black. It appears on the museum's printed material, for instance (*opposite, below*) letterheads, business cards (all printed black on white) and newsletters (printed black with one colour). (Designer: Ryoichi Kondo)

Right: a selection of invitations, all in the same format, for temporary exhibitions. A different colour is selected to identify each event – here (*top to bottom*) brown (Ryoichi Kondo), yellow (Katsumi Asaba), purple (Chihiro Shigeyama), black (Kondo). The text is in black or white. *Below*: leaflet for temporary exhibition. The typography is brown, the event's key colour (see invitation, *top right*). The design was repeated on the catalogue. (Designer: Ryoichi Kondo)

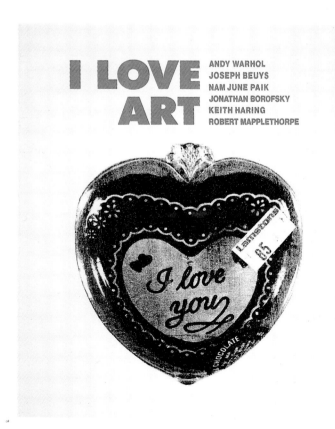

ARTEC
Nagoya

Designer **Dobutsuen Design Office: Satoshi Saito**
Work done **Logo, posters, stationery, merchandise**
Year **1989, 1991**

The first ARTEC exhibition was held in 1989, the second – officially entitled the Second International Biennale in Nagoya – in 1991. ARTEC is founded upon the belief that the role played by technology in art is of great importance (hence its name). Its intentions are to increase public awareness of the possible uses of technology in art; to encourage artists to use it; and to help them to meet people from other countries active in the same field.

The main event is an International Exhibition and Competition for art created using modern technology, such as installation sculpture, interactive computer music, holography, kinetic art and video installation. In 1991, this event was supported by five other major categories. An Open Competition and Exhibition was organized to encourage and promote young artists working with technology. A new section, the Theme Exhibition, was introduced to provide a further insight into art and technology. Performances, including films, were organized in and around the city's art and science museums. An outdoor exhibition of about thirty light-generating works was held in Shirakawa Park, in which the museums stand. Finally, there was a symposium. The Biennale's council is supported by several bodies, including the Aichi Prefecture, Nagoya City and the Chunichi Shimbun (a long-established Japanese newspaper).

After a discussion of all aspects of ARTEC with its organizers, Satoshi Saito created a logo in an exceedingly contemporary style which attracts and intrigues the viewer. By playing with different screens for the image, by cropping and distorting it, the designer generates a vitality which is as vigorous on stationery as on posters and printed material. The colours are brilliant but not vulgar, and this adds to the eye-catching quality of the symbol without distorting the visual imagery's essential nature. More attention could, however, have been devoted to the typography, which is rather too straightforward.

The choice of the eye as a motif encapsulates the Biennale's objective: the presentation of art that must be seen to be appreciated. Saito intends, however, that the eye should represent not merely the viewer – the art on show also views, and criticizes, its viewers.

The contemporary-style logo (*below*) was inspired by the notion of seeing: the eye is both the spectator regarding the art and the art regarding the spectator.

The 2nd International Biennale In Nagoya, 1991

The basic logo undergoes several transformations, created by various technical processes. *Opposite*: letterhead with envelope, news brochure giving information on 1991 events. *Above*: catalogue cover and poster. *Right*: the interior of a Christmas card from the ARTEC Secretariat.

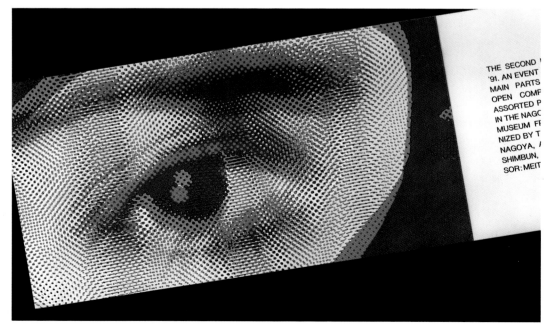

Meguro Museum of Art
Tokyo

Designer **Kijuro Yahagi**
Work done **Logo, stationery, posters, catalogues**
Year **1985**

Meguro City's public art museum, which was opened in November 1987, exhibits modern and contemporary art and design. The museum's objective is the development of a better understanding of the past and present, in order to pursue the possibilities of the future. The main theme of its permanent collection is art created by Japanese artists while staying abroad. These works create a clear bond with Western artistic traditions, but at the same time reveal the unique character of modern Japanese art. In addition, about eight temporary exhibitions are held each year. As well as maintaining its collection, the museum gathers together other materials that are relevant to it – films, photographs, books for its library, educational materials. The museum produces a yearly journal and a newsletter, as well as numerous occasional publications. Its staff organize educational activities such as lectures, workshops to appeal to young and old alike, symposia and demonstrations. The Kumin (or Community) Gallery is not only used for museum exhibitions, but is also available for rent by members of the public.

The logo is a simple letter 'M' made up of four rectangular rods, each of which is created by a narrow black line enclosing a central space; it can also be reversed out in white. It is usually supported by the museum name in Japanese and English, which can be printed either on each side of the logo (English to the left, Japanese to the right) or below it, ranged left or centred. The logo can be framed by a black or grey rectangular panel, or printed directly against the background on which it is being used.

The logo appears in one of its variants on a wide range of museum items, all of which keep to a muted range of colours. There are, for instance, grey carrier bags with black handles; grey protective plastic pouches; white and straw-tinted writing paper, grey and white envelopes in a folder of corrugated card; catalogue jackets in soft shades of green or dusky pink; a slipcase half black, half buff, with a title panel half white, half grey; a visitors' guide. All the material reflects the sobriety and classicism of the museum's visual identity.

Meguro Museum of Art, Tokyo 目黒区美術館

The museum's logo is a letter 'M' made up of four rectangular rods, outlined in either white or black according to the background. The initial is supported by the museum's name in Japanese and English, positioned either below or on either side. The identity's tone is coolly classical.

The logo is applied in a variety of situations, such as on a corrugated buff-coloured folder (*left*) for stationery (*opposite, top right*) – the 'M' appears discreetly in the corner of the envelopes. *Opposite below*: a carrier bag and plastic pouch from the museum shop. *Top left*: slipcase for the catalogue of the museum's opening exhibition, *Swiss Artists in Residence in Japan*. Five artists were invited to work in the museum for about three months.

THE NETHERLANDS

The Zeebelt is a 'squatted' theatre, started by Gert Dumbar in 1985. Since its opening, it has hosted events intended to research the relationship between the fine arts and the theatre, the emphasis being on design. Its principal activities are symposia, which people come from abroad to attend (subjects include Neville Brody, Pierre Bernard and Eastern Europe); a prize for young talent in art school; a four-colour magazine (*Zeezucht*) and various other publications. It has also awarded a prize for the worst architecture in The Hague. About four to six events are held each month, including performances of dance and avant-garde music, lectures (on design and architecture) and plays (one, for instance, was commissioned from two graphic designers). The administration and programme are subsidized by the city council, but sponsorship plays an important role in the theatre's finances.

The theatre's visual communication is dominated by a preference for breathing life into the printed letter and for maintaining the strong typographic culture so characteristic of the Netherlands. The abstraction is non-decorative, while the use of densely filled and empty space and of asymmetrical layouts leads the graphic artists to treat the text as a formal element in the design. Setting the stage for the written word in this way intrigues the viewer to such an extent that reading becomes a pleasurable game, an activity requiring a high level of concentration. The affinity for typography does not exclude the use of visual images, which are employed to act as a stimulus for the imagination. The theatre's graphics and use of imagery reflect the originality of a unique, vibrant centre for the arts.

Zeebelt Theater
The Hague

Designer **Studio Dumbar**
***Work done* Posters, programmes, postcards, magazine**
***Year* 1985–90**

Poster for a symposium, '4 × 2 Visions of Graphic Design', held at the Zeebelt. Each of the four days featured two designers, from Great Britain, Germany, France and the Netherlands. The poster colours are sober: black background, white typography for the title, yellow for the designers' names, red for the theatre, a red text panel with white and black lettering. The colours are reflected in the poster's visuals, which emphasize discussion as the principal activity of the symposium by the portrayal of a range of open, toothy 'mouths'.

Stedelijk Museum
Amsterdam

Designers Daphne + Ben Duijvelshoff van Peski. Hard Werken
Work done Posters, catalogues, periodicals
Year 1988–90

The Stedelijk is Amsterdam's modern art museum, which collects and displays works from 1850 to the present. It was originally founded as the city's municipal museum, the immediate impetus being the need for a gallery to house a legacy of Sophia Augusta de Bruyn. A.W. Weissman's neo-Renaissance building (since altered and added to) was opened in 1895. The de Bruyn legacy occupied one wing, while the rest of the building provided facilities for exhibitions and a wide variety of collections, including that of the Association for Forming a Public Collection of Contemporary Art in Amsterdam. Over the years, the number of contemporary art exhibitions gradually grew and the museum's other collections were relocated elsewhere, until in the early '70s the

Stedelijk finally became exclusively devoted to modern art. It was during the energetic directorship of Willem Sandberg (1945–63) that the museum's exhibition policy and collections became both more daring and more international.

Today, the Stedelijk owns paintings and sculpture, drawings and prints, photographs, videos, posters, industrial design and applied art. It keeps on permanent show its modern 'classics' – Cézanne, Chagall, Manet, Matisse, Monet, Picasso and Van Gogh – and also the fathers of abstract art, Mondrian and Malevich. The current director, Wim Beeren, has made sculpture a striking facet of the museum's acquisitions policy.

The museum organizes a range of activities such as lectures, films, live performances and contemporary music concerts. It also has a comprehensive library, open to the public, which specializes in literature on modern art since 1860.

In the 1960s, under the artistic guidance first of Sandberg and then Wim Crouwel, the Stedelijk was a pioneer in the field of visual identity for museums, with a graphic chart and a highly innovatory alphabet. Nevertheless, at the present time it has no institutional image. It concentrates on commissioning designers to create identities for temporary events but neglects its permanent image – for instance, it does not have a 'designed' letterhead.

Following the tradition established by its strong, pioneering visual image in the 1960s, the Stedelijk's identity is dominated by typography. A minimum of means is employed to convey a maximum of information through strong, architectural images.

Left: poster for an exhibition ('A Great Activity') of work by young Dutch artists. A large and small version were required; the economical solution was to design a large poster that could be tightly cropped to become the small one. (Designer: Hard Werken, Rotterdam)

Opposite: the Stedelijk's lorry and a selection of covers for *Bulletin*, the museum's magazine. (Designer: Daphne + Ben Duijvelshoff van Peski)

Its current graphic designers have adopted an approach composed of two elements: the evaluation of what is essential and the communication of information. This has resulted in a predominantly typographic identity, which is, however, flexible enough to cope with the large variety of subjects required. The guiding principle for museum publications and posters is not to create an advertising splash, but to organize information with clarity by means of typography, which offers enough possibilities to create an image. The posters, catalogue and periodical covers and page layouts provide ample evidence that an effective image can be produced with the minimum of different graphic treatments. What dominates the design is the high value attached to the information it is intended to convey. The typography is not just the way a particular word is printed; it becomes a formal element in the design, pushing up against the boundary of abstraction. The designers' work is inspired by the Swiss school and by the Dutch studio Total Design in its combination of austerity and legibility, but it goes further than either. Quite without fear, the designers employ diverse ranges of decorative elements and distortions of typographic characters.

Through its posters and publications, the Stedelijk achieves a particularly strong image couched in contemporary language while drawing upon traditional graphic tools.

Centraal Museum
Utrecht

Designers Various
Work done Stationery
Year 1990

The Centraal Museum, founded in 1838, is the oldest municipal museum in the Netherlands. Over the years it has developed from a modest historical collection to a large collection containing a wide range of works: fashion and dress; arts and crafts; coins and medals; paintings by Utrecht masters; a floor devoted to the city's history; and an extremely rare Utrecht ship dating from the 12th century. In 1986, the museum converted a stable block into an exhibition room for its collection of 20th-century Dutch art and temporary exhibitions.

In 1990, it was decided to give a face-lift to the institution's visual identity. Instead of inviting a single designer to invent a new corporate image, the museum staff looked at the mass of potential talent in the Netherlands and agreed to take a chance: various designers would be employed to produce different items of stationery. As a result, the identity consists of an anarchy of visual ideas about the museum. By way of humorous emphasis, the project has been dubbed 'No Total Design Style'. The participating designers are: Jan Pinto of Studio Bauman; Gea Grevink; Boudewijn Boer; Annelieke Grob and Olivia Ettema; Edith Gruson and Ewoud Traast; Caroline Zeevat; and Martijn Swart.

At first sight, the effect of all this variety is astonishing. The various different stylistic trends are represented: baroque, Constructivist typography, and so on. There is no graphic chart, no logo. What the designers have produced are interpretations of a variety of themes, which can also be seen as a series of nods in the direction of graphic design. The least important piece of stationery, brochure cover, envelope, invitation card or press announcement becomes a decorative element, a creative gamble. There is no limit to the desire for graphic proliferation. Each theme is the subject of different treatments and forms the basis for a game of infinite variety played with images such as hats and typography. Sometimes the typography is used in such a way that it bubbles over past the sense of the printed word to become a purely formal element. This identity, with its anti-graphic plan outlook and creative freedom, has the functional characteristics of ease of reading and the rapid communication of information.

Examples of stationery commissioned by the Centraal Museum from a host of different designers in pursuit of an anti-graphic plan identity, or 'No Total Design Style'. *Below* : Boudewijn Boer's press-release paper. The museum's name appears in yellow in a red or blue rectangle.

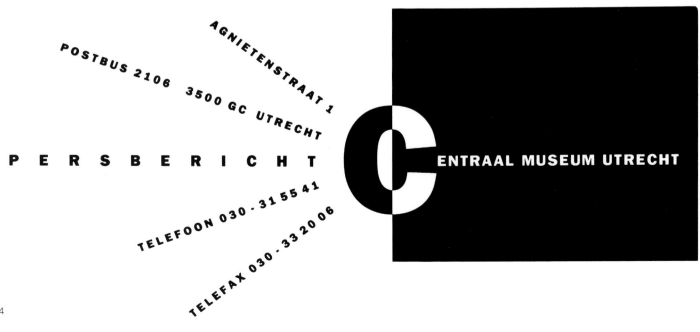

Envelope by Gea Grevink in grey, blue and white.

The reverse side of letter paper, printed scarlet by Caroline Zeevat.

Four-colour letter paper in two designs – costume and silver – by Martijn Swart.

Reverse side of press-release paper: scarlet, maroon and white on turquoise. Annelieke Grob, Olivia Ettema.

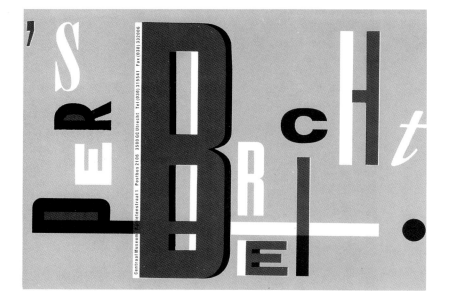

Holland Festival
Amsterdam

Designer Studio Dumbar
Work done Poster, promotional material
Year 1986–90

This avant-garde festival, which was first held in 1948 and is comparable with the Edinburgh Festival, is chiefly concerned with music. Since 1986, it has extended its activities to include the graphic arts, while still maintaining its original objectives: the discovery of new talent and introducing to the public the ideas of the avant-garde. The festival takes places annually in the summer and lasts for one month.

The festival's graphic designers have turned away from the functionalism of the Swiss school and gone back to the principle of old posters: giving the viewers something to read while taking their time; letting them absorb at several readings pieces of scattered but hierarchically organized information. In response to the festival's activities, which require an avant-garde image, the visual programme is a mixture of strict rules and ideas inspired by different contemporary styles. The graphic elements are extremely varied – nothing is out of bounds, nothing held back – but they are deployed with perfect mastery. The result is provocative images which achieve their effect more by playing on the viewer's emotions than by their functionalism.

The guiding principle seems to be to create with every prospectus, magazine, poster or whatever, an item that is in itself innovative, whether entertaining or gloomy, theatrical or musical, according to the event it is advertising. In order to produce these vigorous images, which are sometimes difficult to read, the designers are able to call on all available media: photography, painting, sculpture, paper cut-outs, computer images. This rich, highly personal mode of expression is balanced by a structured typography. Within the studio, responsibility for the work was split, Gert Dumbar and Lex van Pieterson providing the image and others the typography. Their combined effort transmits a passion for art, its languages and creators, and produces a graphic art which is non-derivative.

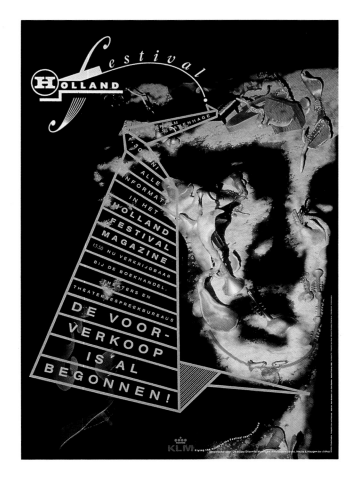

The logo combines letters of different sizes and typefaces to create a flowing, readily recognizable word-pattern. All the documents bring together a highly personal mode of expression and a structured typography. Posters often return to the older principle of presenting the viewer with so much text that it takes time to read it – as the festival is intended mainly for Dutch people, no language problem arises.

Opposite: poster giving information for ticket sales (1988) and magazine cover (1989). *This page*: poster (1986, *above*); inside the preliminary schedule booklet (1987, *above right*); change of address card, compliments slip and address label (1986, *right*).

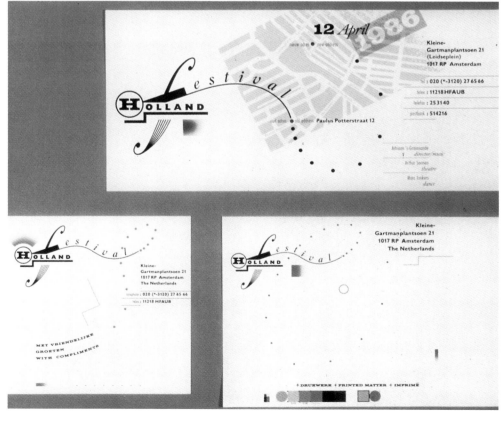

Rijksmuseum
Amsterdam

Designer Studio Dumbar
Work done Stationery, signage, promotional material
Year 1986–87

The foundation of the Rijksmuseum, the national museum of the Netherlands, dates back to Louis Bonaparte's establishing a 'Royal Museum' by decree in 1808. The present building, however, whose architect was P.J.H. Cuypers, was not opened until 1885. Its façades are decorated with reliefs by G. Sturm.

The museum has accumulated an outstanding collection of paintings by the Dutch masters, from the 15th century to the present day. In addition, the permanent collection contains prints; Flemish paintings; works of the Italian Schools; sculpture and applied arts; items relating to Dutch history; and art from Asia. Temporary exhibitions are organized on complementary topics.

In the mid-1980s it was decided to renew the museum's graphic identity and sign system, originally designed in the '60s. What it needed was an image at once elegant – to reflect the age of many of the exhibits – and modern – in keeping with the museum's contemporary character. Its atmosphere led the graphic artists to select a classic typography (Baskerville and News Gothic), combined with a modern approach to design. The relationship between the old and new also forms the basis for the pictograms invented for the sign system, in which modern symbols are adventurously superimposed against details of paintings by Old Masters.

The guiding principles of the sign system are the need for flexibility and cheapness. The text is printed line by line on magnetic strips, so that it can easily be changed as required by museum curators themselves. On permanent signs, information is given in two languages, Dutch and English, directing visitors to different areas of the museum: for instance the applied arts section, the shop, the restaurant, the *Nightwatch*. Key facilities, such as information, toilets and the restaurant, are also indicated by the museum's special pictograms. These overcome the language barrier and are perfectly understood by all the museum's visitors (two million per annum).

The museum's leaflet explaining the floorplan in four languages is given a light-hearted treatment unusual for this type of document. Its tone comes from

The Rijksmuseum's logo (*above*) is deployed prominently on the museum's stationery. Printed in black and white, it unites a classic typography – Baskerville and News Gothic – with a contemporary design approach. Note the 'mirror effect' treatment of the first two and final two letters of '*museum*'.

Opposite : selection of printed materials. *Left* : museum catalogue cover. *Right* : poster for an exhibition of artifacts brought up from a Dutch shipwreck. *Below* : invitation to a farewell celebration on the departure of the head of the Rijksmuseum; *this page, left* : special stationery to mark the same event.

the way in which it is cut and folded, the use of colour and the incorporation of the museum's pictograms.

The administrative stationery makes use of simple typography. There are two variants: black on white and white on black. Either each line of print is separated by a narrow rule, or reversed out letters, skilfully treated, are enclosed within a fine black border.

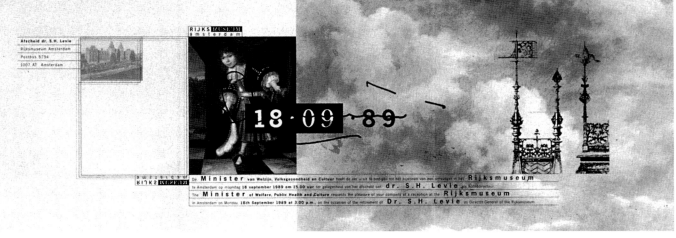

Dumbar's work is important for the way it develops the link between design and the fine arts. He actually uses art for design (the Rijksmuseum pictograms, for instance). His comments on the process are illuminating: 'I expect that new tendencies in the fine arts will have great influence on the creative values of our profession in the near future. In particular those tendencies which take place at the interface of fine art and design. Conversely, there are numerous objects that belong to the category "design" that claim the autonomy of an artistic object. In my opinion this tendency will be the most important and energetic influence on international graphic design in the next decade.'

RIJKSMUSEUM

Right: the pictograms for the sign system superimpose modern symbols against details of paintings by Old Masters, a daring idea which works very well. *Below right*: a sign *in situ* in the museum.

A series of posters for exhibitions put on by the Rijksmuseum's old prints department (*opposite*) and a poster for a show about picture frames (*below*).

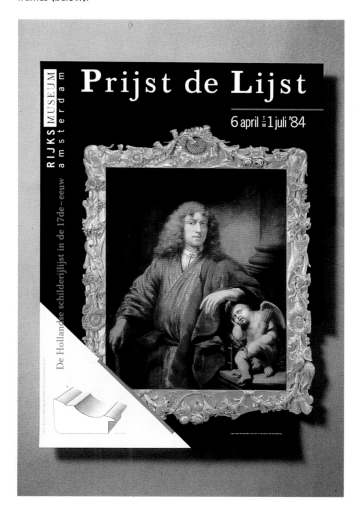

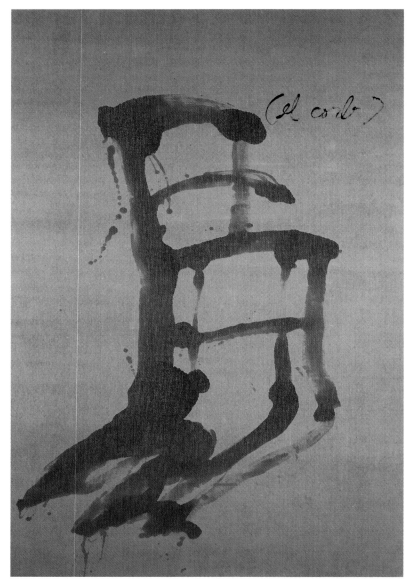

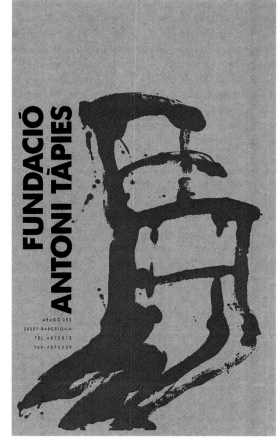

**FUNDACIÓ
ANTONI TÀPIES**

ARAGÓ 255

08007 BARCELONA

TEL. 4870315

FAX 4870009

/300 × 200 cm, varnish on canvas). Red-brown was chosen because it is often used by Tàpies and because it echoes the red bricks of the museum building.

The adoption of a strong Tàpies image to symbolize the collection means that in effect the designers are inviting visitors to acquire for themselves the artist's work in the form of bags, posters, invitations, T-shirts, or whatever. By reproducing an actual work of art, the designers have created an identity that delivers a direct message about the nature of the institution but at the same time is used unobtrusively, like a signature in the corner of a painting, without damaging in any way the spirit of the original.

FUNDACIO ANTONI TAPIES

The initial idea for the institution's symbol came from Tàpies's aluminium-tube sculpture of clouds surmounted by a chair, which rises above the façade of Domènech i Montaner's 19th-century building (*right*). The mark is actually derived, however, from Tàpies's painting *Gran Cadira* (*opposite, far left*). The designers have created an image suitable for a multitude of situations – from paper bags (*opposite, above right*) and stationery to T-shirts (*opposite below* and *below*) – without in any way diminishing the original painting.

ARCO: Feria Internacional de Arte Contemporáneo
Madrid

Designer CR Communication & Design Services: Carlos Rolando
Work done Logo, stationery, promotional material
Year 1986–91

ARCO, Madrid's contemporary art fair (*AR*te *CO*ntemporáneo), was first held in 1982. The following decade has seen the event's international ambitions increase in size and become more closely defined, the driving force being a real wish to support Spain's growing young arts scene. The fair has issued more invitations to foreign galleries, it has organized cultural events such as colloquia and given its name to the ARCO Foundation, which acquires contemporary art from galleries exhibiting at the fair. The fair is popular and enjoys an excellent reputation as a place to buy art; more than 100,000 visitors came in 1989.

Carlos Rolando's identity was designed to communicate the event's openness of attitude to artistic trends and to convey the sense of a modern space in which arts people can interact with one another. The space is represented by a square, a shape chosen to accommodate the four letters of ARCO, one in each corner. For the typography, a classic stencil was selected, because it has an artistic quality and produces a 'hand-printed' impression – this may account for its frequent use by artists, mostly Cubists. The stencil has, moreover, an 'open' design – even the 'O' is 'opened up' by splitting it into two halves. A palpable space is created within the bounds of each letter by thickening them, so that the existence of their interiors is emphasized. In addition, placing the letters in the corners of the square creates a 'walk-through' space between them, common to them all.

After creating the logo plan, the colours were chosen. The designer opted for an obvious scheme: red or brown letters on a yellow 'floor' with strong black corners. A twin square of equal size to indicate the year of the event was also included in the identity. In addition, the year can be placed in the middle of the 'Arco' square. The identity was later extended to all the different aspects of the fair, for instance the Amigos de Arco ('Friends of Arco') association, which operates throughout the year. The visual concept of 'corners' is used on every collateral graphic item designed to meet the Fair's need: brochures, newspapers, decorations and so on.

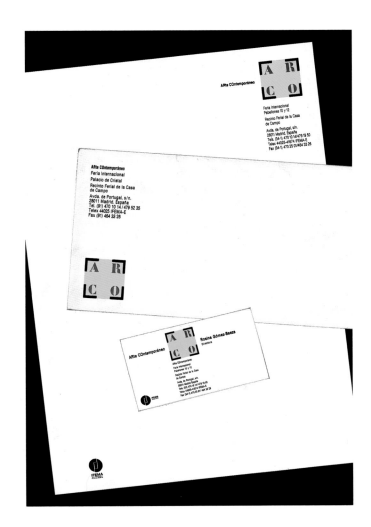

The identity consists of ARCO's name reproduced in classic stencil letters within a square, bounded by black corners. It is intended to represent a contemporary, open space where people can meet to interact with each other and with art.

The basic concept can be varied each year to produce a striking image which nevertheless clearly belongs to the same family. *This page*: posters from 1987 to 1989. *Opposite*: the variants of the square for 1991 and a selection of stationery.

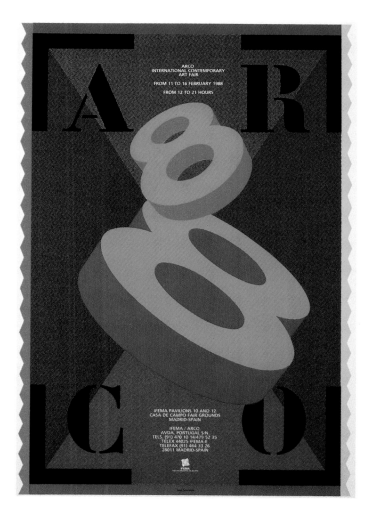

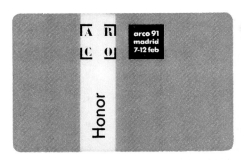

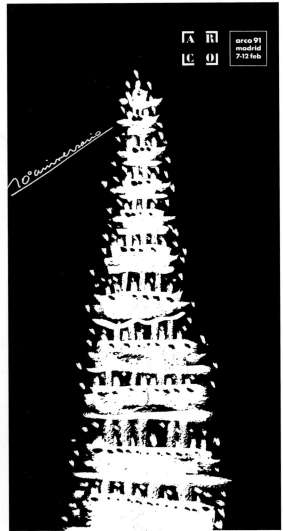

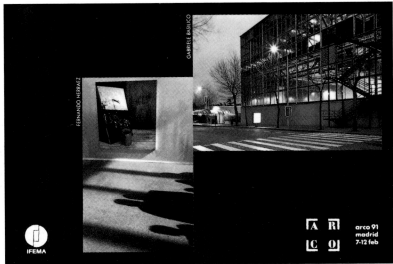

[A R / C O]

arco 91
madrid
7-12 feb

ARCO Feria Internacional
de Arte Contemporáneo
Recinto Ferial
de la Casa de Campo
Pabellones 10 y 12

Avenida de Portugal s/n
28011 Madrid España
Tels. (34 - 1) 470 10 14/479 19 50
Fax (34 - 1) 470 25 01/464 33 26
Telex 44025/41674 IFEMA-E

ARCO

Opposite: a sample of material for the 1991 fair, all carrying the ARCO square.

Right: a forest of ARCO banners.

Fundació Joan Miró
Barcelona

Designers Joan Miró (logo), Yves Zimmerman (stationery)
Work done Stationery, publishing programme
Year 1975

After the important retrospective held in Barcelona in 1968 to celebrate Miró's seventy-fifth birthday, the artist agreed to the suggestion that an institution should be set up, with the objective of making accessible to the public not only Miró's own work, but also the principal trends of 20th-century art. In 1975, the resulting Foundation opened its doors. The plans for the building were drawn up by Josep Lluís Sert, who had been a friend of Miró for many years. It is an open-plan structure, constructed in such a way that the maximum natural light enters from above without casting shadows or shining directly onto the works of art. The building material is reinforced concrete, treated so that it is a Mediterranean white rather than grey. Thanks to the bond forged between interior and exterior by the central patio and apertures to the outside, the building creates a perfect balance between architecture and landscape. In 1988 an extension designed by Jaume Freixa was opened.

The permanent collection contains a large number of Miró's works, donated by the artist and others, which are complemented by a small number of pieces by other 20th-century artists (for instance Duchamp, Matisse, Chillida, Rauschenberg). In addition, the Foundation organizes activities for school children, recitals of contemporary music, lectures, seminars and temporary exhibitions on 20th-century trends and artists.

The logo, an abstract design typical of Miró's work, was created by the artist in 1975 for the institution. The stationery was by Yves Zimmermann, a Swiss designer who lives in Barcelona. The logo is increased or decreased in size to take up the full width of headed paper, calling cards, letter pads and so on. In counterpoint to the freehand motif, bold Univers typography is printed in three columns, in red and black. The ensemble achieves immediate recognition, while according full respect to Miró's drawing.

The graphics employed for the series of museum leaflets give them a high-quality appearance: elongated formats, the logo either partially or completely reversed out against a background in a primary colour, the consistent use of a single typeface.

Above: detail of the Fundació Joan Miró's logo. ***Opposite, above***: range of letterheads with a business card.
The logo can be used in an enlarged, cropped version. ***Below***: information leaflets, the logo partially or fully
reversed out.

Fundació Joan Miró · Centre d'Estudis d'Art Contemporani · Parc de Montjuïc · 08004 Barcelona · Tel. (93) 329 19 08 · Fax (93) 329 86 09

Fundació Joan Miró · Centre d'Estudis d'Art Contemporani · Parc de Montjuïc · 08004 Barcelona

Fundació Joan Miró · Centre d'Estudis d'Art Contemporani · Parc de Montjuïc · 08004 Barcelona

Fundació Joan Miró · Centre d'Estudis d'Art Contemporani · Parc de Montjuïc · 08038 Barcelona · Tel. (93) 329 19 08

Rosa Maria Malet
Directora

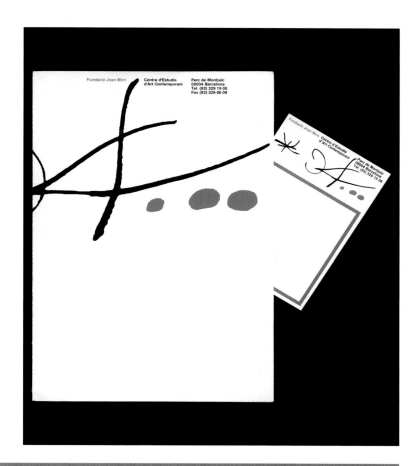

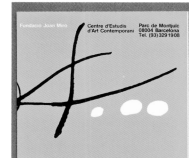
Fundació Joan Miró · Centre d'Estudis d'Art Contemporani · Parc de Montjuïc · 08004 Barcelona · Tel. (93) 329 19 08

**L'art contemporani
a l'abast**

octubre - desembre 1989

Fundació Joan Miró · Centre d'Estudis d'Art Contemporani · Parc de Montjuïc · 08004 Barcelona · Tel. (93) 329 19 08

**Cinema
a la Fundació**

octubre - desembre 1989

Fundació Joan Miró · Centre d'Estudis d'Art Contemporani · Parc de Montjuïc · 08004 Barcelona · Tel. (93) 329 19 08

**Música
a la Fundació**

desembre 1989 - juliol 1990

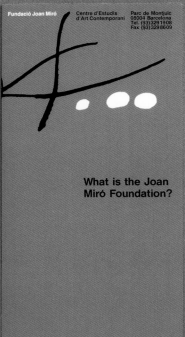
Fundació Joan Miró · Centre d'Estudis d'Art Contemporani · Parc de Montjuïc · 08004 Barcelona · Tel. (93) 329 19 08 · Fax (93) 329 86 09

**What is the Joan
Miró Foundation?**

SWITZERLAND

Musée International de la Croix-Rouge, Geneva

153

Musée International de la Croix-Rouge
Geneva

The Musée International de la Croix-Rouge et du Croissant-Rouge (Red Cross and Red Crescent) tells the story of those men and women who have devoted a part of their lives to helping victims of the major events of our era. It is run by a private foundation under the supervision of the Swiss Federation Authorities.

The three-storeyed building, designed by architects Pierre Zoelly, Georges Haefeli and Michel Girardet, is particularly original in its use of concrete, glass and light. It contains a permanent exhibition, designed by Roger Pfund's studio, areas for temporary exhibitions and an auditorium.

The permanent exhibition, laid out over an area of 2,200 square yards (1,850 square metres), employs state-of-the-art audiovisual techniques. In interpreting the exhibition's themes, extensive and lively use is made of typography in different forms. In addition, works have been commissioned from artists such as Carl Bucher, Georges Segal and Alexandre Meylan.

The institution's identity, which is very strong, has no logo. Recognition is achieved instead through the typographic system, elegant and sober, with text arranged in two or three columns, strengthened by a vertical rule. Administrative stationery is printed in three languages (French, German and English), in red and black on white 'Quovadis' paper.

Guides and documents are noteworthy for the high-quality iconography of their photographs, which are close cropped and printed as bleeds. Above the photograph is a white strip on which practical information is set out. The combined effect is one of great visual power, which reflects a perfect mastery of text and image, together with the blending of the artistic and academic. The use of a standard typography and grid for all documents has created a swiftly recognizable identity and given rise to excellent functional images.

Designers Communication Visuelle: Sophie and Roger Pfund. With Les Ateliers du Nord: Antoine Cahen and Claude Frossard (designers); Roland Aeschlimann (exhibition graphics and staging)
Work done Typographic system for stationery, brochures etc. Exhibition graphics
Year 1988–91

The museum guide is in four languages. Each is distinguished by the use of a powerful, tightly cropped black-and-white photograph. Each follows the museum's consistent typographic system in red and black, including the characteristic vertical rule.

Guide

Il Museo Internazionale della Croce Rossa

La Croce Rossa e la Mezzaluna Rossa attraverso 125 anni di storia

Guide

The International Museum of the Red Cross

The Red Cross and Red Crescent through 125 years of history

Guide

Musée International de la Croix-Rouge

La Croix-Rouge et le Croissant-Rouge à travers 125 ans d'histoire

Guide

Das Internationale Museum des Roten Kreuzes

125 Jahre Geschichte des Roten Kreuzes und des Roten Halbmonds

153

Musée International de la Croix-Rouge et du Croissant-Rouge

Musée international de la Croix-Rouge	Internationales Museum des Roten Kreuzes	International Museum of the Red Cross
Histoire du mouvement de la Croix-Rouge et du Croissant-Rouge	Geschichte der Bewegung des Roten Kreuzes und des Roten Halbmondes	History of the Red Cross and Red Crescent movement

MUSEE INTERNATIONAL DE LA CROIX-ROUGE

The museum has no symbol. Instead recognition is achieved by the use of a standard typography and grid, in which the text is divided into two or three columns, strengthened by a vertical rule.

Opposite : the exterior of the building. Detail from the trilingual letterhead. Museum leaflet showing exhibition areas.

This page : examples of the designers' effective use of photography.

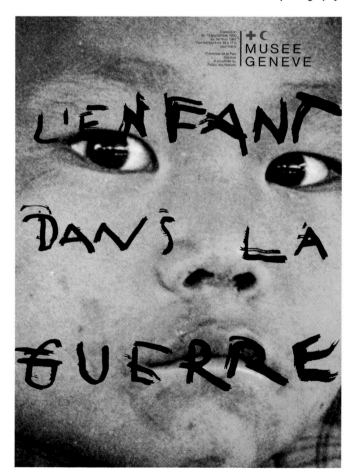

UNITED KINGDOM

The Design Museum, which was opened in 1989, occupies a reconstructed 1950s warehouse beside the River Thames. An extra storey was added to increase the floor space, but the original terraces overlooking the river were retained. The architects, Conran Roche, worked with Stanton Williams on the exhibition spaces to create a functional feel inspired by the Bauhaus.

Its chief mission is to act as a showcase for industrial design, past, present and future, from both a cultural and commercial perspective. Design is examined in the context of its everyday environment, to reveal its effect on the quality of life and its social and economic implications.

Several different groups of designers have worked on various projects. The administrative stationery makes a point of using the museum's geographical location and architecture. On the back of its letter paper (designed by Flo Bayley), a map of the area is printed in pale grey. On the front, a black, grey and white architectural diagram of the building, small (0.9 × 0.6 in/2.2 × 1.6 cm) but perfectly clear, is reproduced next to the address, which employs 1950s-style typography.

Institutional documents intended for the public usually have photographs of the building and are printed in black, grey and red.

In some of the museum's periodicals, the text is superimposed on a background of muted colours. Without repeating the logo, the identity is affirmed by a style which uses typographical games to form word images. Employing an economy of methods, these magazines, which include *Issue* and *Bulletin*, achieve high-quality layouts and iconography.

Design Museum
London

Designers Flo Bayley. Carter Wong. Wolff Olins
Work done Stationery, magazine, leaflets, posters
Year 1988–90

The permanent stationery by Flo Bayley uses an axonometric drawing of the building, complemented by the use of a Gill typeface. A Wolff Olins/Hall poster based on the museum building.

DESIGN MUSEUM

Collection
Exhibitions
Talks
Films
Library
Cafe

The Design Museum at Butlers Wharf is on the River Thames south east of Tower Bridge.

Tuesday to Sunday 11.30am to 6.30pm Closed Monday, open Bank Holidays.

£2, £1 concessions

Design Museum Butlers Wharf Shad Thames London SE1 2YD

01-407 6261

Ferry shuttle from Tower Pier to Butlers Wharf

London Bridge and Tower Hill

London Bridge

BULLETIN
DESIGN MUSEUM

The Great Exhibition (1851)

NUMBER I **JUNE 1989**

DESIGN MUSEUM

Membership DESIGN MUSEUM

DESIGN MUSEUM

Designed by Carter Wong. Photography by Keith Parry. Printed by Jakon Printers. Paper supplies by Wiggins Teape Company.

Kandem night light, Marianne Brandt / Hin Bredendieck, 1928.

An international centre of design
and everyday life

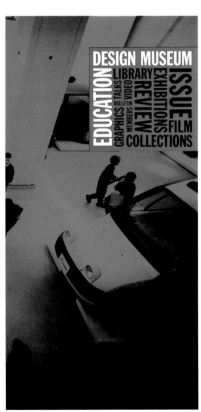

DESIGN MUSEUM
EDUCATION
GRAPHICS LIBRARY TALKS VIDEO BULLETIN MEMBERS REVIEW EXHIBITIONS ISSUE FILM COLLECTIONS

You are invited to
a Champagne Reception
for the opening of

Butlers Wharf
Shad Thames
London SE1 2YD
01-403 6933
RSVP using
enclosed reply card

FRENCH DESIGN
AT THE DESIGN MUSEUM
THURSDAY 2 NOVEMBER 7·30 - 9·30 pm

The Design Museum's
ferry runs between
Tower Pier
(Tower Hill) ⊖
and Butlers Wharf
from 6·50pm

PRIVATE VIEW GENEROUSLY SUPPORTED BY LOUIS VUITTON, SPONSORS OF "DESIGN FRANCAIS 1960-1990 TROIS DECENNIES"

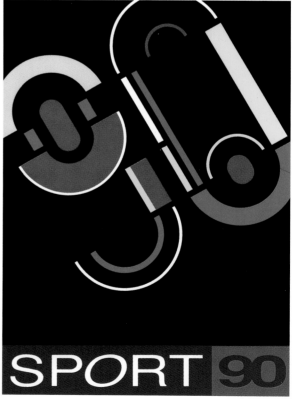

DESIGN MUSEUM

A variety of the museum's documents. *Opposite, far left*: the first issue
of *Bulletin. Centre*: basic information leaflets by Carter Wong. *Right
above*: membership application leaflet (Wolff Olins/Hall), and *below*:
leaflet on the museum's educational facilities (Hayes-Watkins).

This page, above: cover of *Issue* for Autumn 1990 (Wolff Olins/Hall).
The magazine is notable for the high quality of its layout and
illustrations. *Right*: invitations to temporary exhibitions.

Design Council
London

Designer Pentagram: Alan Fletcher and Paul Anthony; David Hillman
Work done Logo, stationery, magazine, booklet
Year 1978, 1987, 1989

The Design Council is a grant-aided body under the Department of Trade and Industry which was set up 'to promote by all practicable means the improvement of design in the products of British industry'. By operating through a network of regional offices, the Council offers a wide range of services to industry and education. These include information and advice on design problems, materials selection, training requirements, management of the design process and technology. The London Design Council has its own exhibition and information centre which caters for wide-ranging and specialist interests in industry, commerce and education, as well as being open to the general public. The Council also runs an awards programme, including the prestigious British Design Awards and the Engineering Design Prize. In addition, the Council is a recognized publishing house, producing, for instance, the annual *Directory of Designers*.

The Design Council's logo, created by Alan Fletcher and Paul Anthony of Pentagram in 1978, successfully combines two different typefaces, both upper case. This, together with printing 'Design' in much heavier type and isolating it by lines above and below, cleverly emphasizes the institution's goal – design – by separating it from 'The . . . Council'. The logo is reproduced on administrative stationery in red and on all Council documents in black and white; it is always easy to read.

Pentagram's David Hillman was responsible for designing two of the Design Council's publications: *The Big Paper* and *D*.

In the spring of 1987, the Design Council's Primary Education Working Party proposed that a magazine should be produced for primary schools in order to encourage design-related activities in the classroom. The result was *The Big Paper* (so-called because of its size), a magazine for primary school teachers and children published three times a year. *The Big Paper*'s logo is a collage of large letter shapes in bright, 'young' colours. A version for black-and-white reproduction was also developed. The typefaces used inside the magazine were specifically selected for ease of word identification. The text is

Right: cover for the first issue of *D* (autumn 1989), a paper for students and staff in higher education.

The Council's logo (*below*) focuses on the institution's goal – design – by the use of two different typefaces, by the boldness of the type and by the insertion of horizontal lines.

THE
DESIGN
COUNCIL

set in Bembo, a serifed face, the headlines in Futura, chosen because it is closest to the logo's letter shapes. Although Futura is non-serifed, it is easy to read because it is set large.

D, a paper for students and staff in higher education, again published three times a year, was launched in 1989. The logo appeared on the launch poster and booklet, both by Hillman. The booklet (4 × 5.7 in/10.5 × 14.5 cm) features on each left-hand page a different image incorporating a 'D'; on the right is a short text built around an associated word beginning with 'D' – for instance 'design', 'degree', 'Dostoevsky', 'different', 'details'.

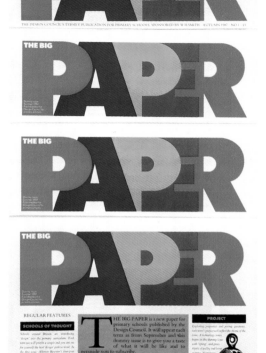

Right: dummy issue to publicize *The Big Paper* (summer 1987). The bright, large letters of the logo are designed to appeal to primary school children.

Spreads from the interior of the launch booklet for *D* (*below*). Each left-hand page bears a different image built around 'D', each right-hand page a text built around letters beginning with 'D'.

Details of the first **D** are being finalised right now. There will be a theme for each issue - the 1990s, jobs, design management, the environment and so on. Features include student work, professional design, industry links, new technology, business, overseas design,

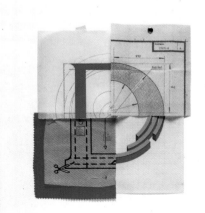

Design is not art, and it's not science. Design is beginning to be recognised as a different kind of subject. That's why **D** is being published now. It will champion the cause of student designers - and the cause of design itself. Whether you are in a foundation course or your final year - studying graphics, product design, interiors, fashion or textiles - **D** is for you. **D** is for design.

Victoria and Albert Museum
London

Designer Pentagram: Alan Fletcher
Work done Logo, sign system
Year 1989

The *Mobil Guide to the Museum* succinctly introduces the visitor to the institution's collections: 'The Victoria and Albert Museum is the home of the world's greatest collection of applied art and design. Its galleries reflect centuries of achievement in such varied fields as ceramics, furniture, jewellery, metalwork, textiles and dress – not only from Europe but also from the Far East, South Asia and the Islamic World. The V & A also contains the national collections of sculpture, watercolours, portrait miniatures and photography, as well as the National Art Library.'

A very large structure is needed to house such an extensive treasury. Consequently the Cromwell Road edifice, opened in 1909 by Edward VII, is a complex maze of galleries which has been added to many times. Pentagram's sign system for this confusing building is based on a colour compass: red for north, green for south, blue for west and yellow for east. Colour-coded banners at the entrance to each gallery show visitors where they are and in which direction they are going. The signs are linked to a colour-coded map, distributed free. The map, together with the simple system of banners, makes it easy for visitors to find their way through the seven miles of galleries.

The logotype of the Victoria and Albert Museum, also designed by Pentagram, uses the original 18th-century typeface of Giambattista Bodoni. The 'A' is reduced to just the right-hand stroke, and the mark is invested with its distinctive personality by the substitution of the upper arm of the ampersand for the left-hand stroke and cross-bar of the 'A'.

The administrative stationery is printed in grey for the logo, red for the address, on white Ingres paper. The wide range of museum publications always reproduce the logo in an appropriate dominant colour; they are, however, too numerous for discussion here.

The museum entrusts to various designers the graphics work for its temporary exhibitions, conferences and so on. This has the effect of shattering its identity, which is visible only in the logo.

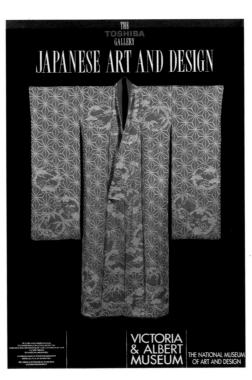

Pentagram's logo is particularly distinctive for the way in which the left stroke and the cross-bar of the 'A' are replaced by the upper arm of the ampersand.

A selection of posters by various designers to advertise exhibitions at the museum. Those *opposite* predate the introduction of the Pentagram identity. *Right*: the pictorial imagery of the later posters is extremely varied, but the logo acts to some extent as a unifying mechanism.

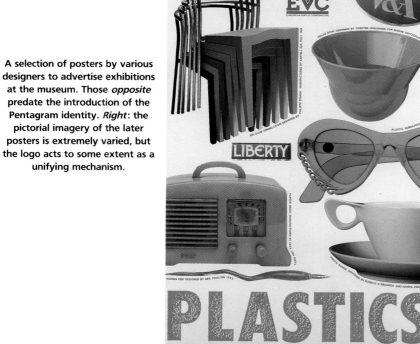

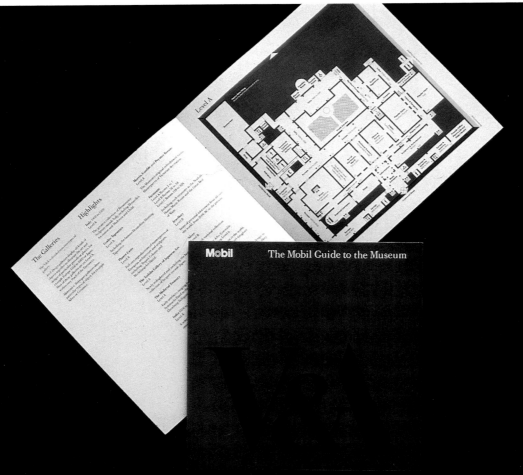

The 18th-century typeface of Giambattista Bodoni is used for the logo. Here it is reproduced in black on a grey carpet, in pale grey on a jacket pocket, and in black on rich brown on the cover of the *Mobil Guide to the Museum.*

VICTORIA AND ALBERT MUSEUM

Pentagram adopted a colour-coded compass for their sign system to help visitors find their way around a huge, rambling building. Red represents north, green south, blue west and yellow east.

Right : blue exhibition banners.

Imperial War Museum
London

Designer Minale, Tattersfield & Partners: Brian Tattersfield (artistic director), Gillian Hodgson (designer)
Work done Logo, stationery, brochure, sign system
Year 1989

The Imperial War Museum is the United Kingdom's national museum dealing with 20th-century conflict, from 1914 to the present day. Its subject is not just military life, but the way in which war affects civilization as a whole. It has a collection of about 10,000 paintings, drawings and sculptures as well as military objects: uniforms, logbooks, newspapers, postcards, letters, diaries and so on. The main museum building, which was extensively redeveloped at the end of the 1980s by Arup Associates, was once the old Bedlam Hospital.

The chief problem in formulating the museum's identity was to avoid glorifying war. The logo is based on the initials 'W' and 'M', formed by searchlights against a background of earth, sea and sky, symbolic of the army, navy and air force. A further allusion is made to the services by the use of their colours: green for the army, blue for the navy and airforce. The logo serves not just the main museum in Lambeth, but also its outposts elsewhere in London and in Cambridge, and is used on everything connected with the institution: stationery, staff uniforms, vehicle liveries, and so on.

The museum signs are made of a mixture of motifs suggesting military insignia, the differing styles of the letters being drawn from its collection. The signs for the café and shop are enamelled. All colours, whether on institutional documents or on signs, are printed solid.

The identity, which derives great power from its concerted effect, won the *DesignWeek* Award for corporate identity in 1990 and appears to have increased considerably the number of visitors to the museum.

The logo manages to avoid glorifying war, while at the same time referring to conflict and the armed forces. The museum's initials, 'WM', are formed by the beams of searchlights which travel across the armed forces' areas of responsibility – land, sea and sky. The colours of the army (green), navy (blue) and air force (blue) are present in the colours of the landscape.

Some of the varied applications of the logo.

The museum signs are put together from a mixture of motifs which suggest military insignia. The letters are drawn from items in the permanent collection.

Third Eye Centre
Glasgow

Designer **Westpoint Design Consultants**
Work done **Logo, stationery, sign system**
Year **1990**

The Third Eye Centre is a Glaswegian cultural institution dedicated to presenting new developments in the visual and performing arts. It has no permanent collection, but regularly commissions artists in such widely varying fields as the plastic arts, theatre, music, dance and design.

Founded in 1973, the centre moved to its present home in Sauchiehall Street in 1975, where it occupies part of the Grecian Chambers of the Victorian architect, Alexander 'Greek' Thomson. The buildings, erected in 1865, are an important example of Thomson's commercial architecture. They were in serious disrepair when acquired by Third Eye, but have been extensively converted and refurbished both inside and out. Now restored to its former

magnificence, the building (floodlit at night) is one of the outstanding architectural features of its busy street. The public areas inside are designed to create a relaxing and welcoming atmosphere for visitors.

The logo is made up of three arcs from a circle, each of a different width, and is intended to suggest ideas of the circle and the centre. It always appears with the centre's name as a caption. On the stationery (white Ingres paper), the logo is printed in purple, red and gold. Practical information appears in grey at the bottom right, centred directly below the logo. This is an unusual arrangement which makes it difficult for the typist to position the letter correctly on the page.

An important factor in the choice of logo was simplicity: only a very simple graphic device could echo the centre's artistic impartiality. It is important that it should not align itself with any artistic style. And yet in spite of the need for a degree of abstraction and neutrality the design does not operate exclusively on an abstract level: a resemblance to an 'eye' and the idea of 'three' has been kept in order to render the meaning of the logo less universal and more particular to the Third Eye Centre.

Other aspects of the centre's corporate identity have been developed in addition to the logo. These are built around two elements: typefaces and colours. Two type families, Futura Condensed and Joanna, form the core

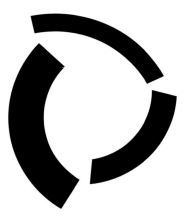

THIRD EYE CENTRE

The visual identity rests upon three foundations: logo, colour and typefaces. The logo, made up of arcs from three circles in purple, red and gold, suggests the centre within a circle, as well as a stylized eye. One of its numerous applications: a window banner (*left*).

material of all the Third Eye's publications and signage. The colours selected for the identity are gold, crimson, blue-purple and grey. Gold appears in the use of natural wood in the centre; red and purple are used in certain finishes, mainly flooring and soft furnishing, grey for all signage areas including noticeboards. The colours are put to most vivid use in the café.

The centre has preferred not to be the prisoner of over-strict identity rules. Many of its publications, for instance various programmes of events and a visitors' guide, are designed in-house on an Apple Mac, following the typographic guidelines of the external designers.

The sign system incorporates the logo, printed either solid or gloss. A system of horizontal bars from which posters and so on can be suspended at different levels is used to convey information. This recalls trends from the '60s and '70s and the grand era of performing art.

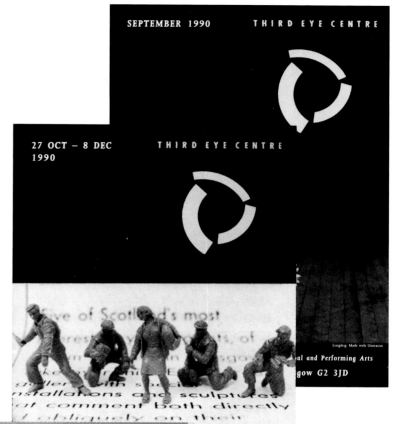

A selection of museum leaflets which were designed in-house, following the typographic guidelines worked out by Westpoint Design Consultants. The two programme covers (*above*) are black with white typography, black-and-white photographs, the logos in yellow (September) and gold/orange (October/December). By contrast the Mayfest programme cover (*left*) has fluorescent pink letters, shadowed with turquoise, on a white ground. The typography is either black or white, reversed out.

Museum of Modern Art
Oxford

Designer Pentagram: Mervyn Kurlansky
Work done Logotype, sign system, posters
Year 1987

The Museum of Modern Art (MOMA), Oxford, which celebrated its twenty-fifth anniversary in 1990, has won a considerable reputation for its pioneering exhibitions. During the 1960s and early '70s, MOMA became Britain's foremost 'Alternative Space'. From the mid-'70s, its programme has been broadened to take in all aspects of 20th-century art, with emphasis on other cultures.

The museum is housed in a converted Victorian brewery and it was the building's architecture, with its metal columns and structured layout, that inspired the linear pattern of its new identity. By combining typography with pattern, the logotype – and the sign system, for which the same approach was adopted – graphically echo the building's columns and decorations.

When creating the identity, Pentagram did not merely design the logotype; they went on to make it into a word-image for use in all contexts. Extremely architectural in construction and employing sober typography, the logo is easily read wherever and in whatever form it appears, whether as white lettering on black or white lettering against strong, basic colours – red, blue, green or yellow. An extra black modern typeface was chosen to provide dramatic contrast for the name.

Pentagram initially designed a system of different coloured logos (with black lettering for the addresses) for the letterheads to differentiate between departments: red, with its connotations of excitement, for press release paper (and address labels); green for fundraising letters from the development department; blue for compliment slips; black for formal museum letterheads and general correspondence. Blue letterheads for the education department were never produced. Although the museum liked the scheme, the expense means that reprints are usually done in uniform black.

Once the visual identity and sign systems were successfully completed, Pentagram was commissioned to undertake poster designs for the museum's temporary exhibitions. At first the museum staff were reluctant to move away from showing works from the exhibitions on the posters, but they were gradually persuaded of the effectiveness of a purely graphic solution.

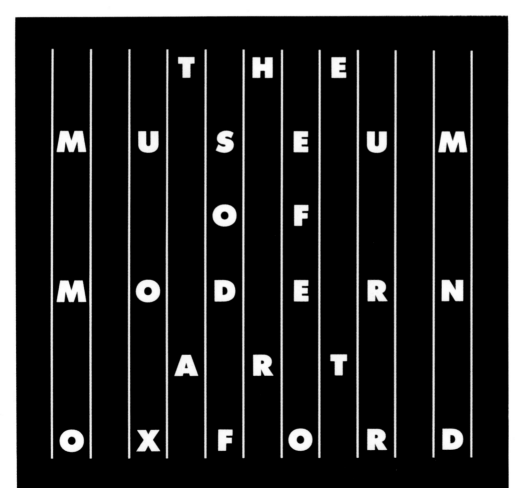

The logo echoes in graphic form the metal columns of the museum building. Black can be replaced by brilliant colours.

Logo applications (*opposite*): stationery, with Pentagram's original colour coding, invitations and carrier bags.

President
Lord Goodman

Chairman
Louis van Praag

Vice Chairman
Nicholas Mann

Treasurer
Peter Alcock

Company Secretary
Brian Jefferson

Director
David Elliott

Name

Valid until end

3P Telephone: 0865 722733 Fax: 0865 726753 Telex: M!

PRIVATE VIEW

Makonde: Wooden Sculpture
from East Africa
From the Malde Collection
2 April–21 May 1989

You are invited to the Private View
Saturday 1 April 6–8pm

Exhibition organised by The Museum
of Modern Art Oxford

The Museum of Modern Art Oxford
30 Pembroke Street
Oxford OX1 1BP

The Museum of Modern Art receives
financial assistance from the Arts
Council of Great Britain, Oxford City
Council, Oxfordshire County
Council, Visiting Arts and Southern
Arts.

PRIVATE VIEW

Sue Coe : Police State
22 January – 26 March 1989

Private view
21 January 1989 6–8pm

The exhibition was organised
by Marilyn Zeitlin at the
Anderson Gallery, Richmond
Virginia, USA in conjunction
with Sally Baker, New York and
The Museum of Modern
Art Oxford.

The Museum of Modern Art Oxford
receives financial assistance from
The Arts Council of Great Britain,
Oxford City Council,
Oxfordshire County Council,
Visiting Arts and
Southern Arts.

LICHTENSTEIN

'64

The Drawings of Roy Lichtenstein
22 May – 3 July 1988
The Museum of Modern Art Oxford
30 Pembroke Street
Oxford OX1 1BP
Recorded information (0865) 728608
Tuesday to Saturday 10am – 6pm
Sunday 2 – 6pm Monday closed
Admission: minimum 50p
Friends and concessions free
The exhibition was organised under the
auspices of The International Council of
The Museum of Modern Art, New York,
and is presented with the assistance of
the Henry J. and Drue Heinz Foundation.
The Museum of Modern Art Oxford
receives financial assistance from
the Arts Council of Great Britain,
Oxford City Council, Oxfordshire
County Council and Visiting Arts.

The Museum of Modern Art Oxford
30 Pembroke Street Oxford OX1 1BP
Recorded information (0865) 728608
Admission £1, Concessions 50p, Friends free.
The Museum of Modern Art Oxford
receives financial assistance from
The Arts Council of Great Britain,
Oxford City Council, Oxfordshire County
Council, Visiting Arts, Southern Arts.

Makonde: Wooden
Sculpture from East Africa
From the Malde Collection
2 April – 21 May 1989

OPENING
TIMES

MUSEUM AND SHOP
TUESDAY – SATURDAY 10 A.M. – 6 P.M.
SUNDAY 2 P.M. – 6 P.M.

CAFE MOMA
TUESDAY – SATURDAY 10 A.M. – 5 P.M.
SUNDAY 2 P.M. – 5 P.M.

OFFICES AND DELIVERIES AT REAR
IN ST. EBBE'S YARD

MUSEUM OF MODERN ART, OXFORD

Following the success of the visual identity and sign systems, Pentagram was commissioned to design posters for temporary exhibitions. With time, the museum staff were persuaded to move away from focusing on an exhibition item (*opposite, left*, 1988) to a purely graphic image (*opposite, right* 1989).

The sign system (*right* and *opposite, below right*) adopts and adapts the image of the logo and is based on black.

A clever play on the logo: coloured pencils in a box on sale in the museum shop (*opposite, below left*).

Eureka! The Children's Museum
Halifax

Designer **Pentagram: Mervyn Kurlansky**
Work done **Logo, brochure**
Year **1987–90**

Eureka! will be the first learning centre for 5- to 11-year-olds established by the educational charity, the Children's Museum. The project was originally put forward in 1983, and the museum's new building should open in Halifax in 1992.

It will be the first institution of its kind in the United Kingdom, and 'Learning through fun' could serve as its motto. Its goal is to enhance the physical and mental development of children through 'hands-on' experiences in an interactive environment. Without being a substitute for schools, the museum is intended to give parents and teachers the opportunity of enriching children's learning processes, both technical and artistic.

The name and logotype, which won a silver award at the New York Art Directors Club in May 1988, were both Pentagram inventions designed to express the theme of discovery. The playful logo consists of letters formed from rods and draws its inspiration from the building game for children played with sticks in primary colours.

The project's presentation brochure is illustrated with pictures executed in a child-like style and, by the simple device of cutting a window in the middle of the page, reading it is turned into a game of discovery. The text is justified and the typography is very easy to read, thanks to the way the first letter of each sentence is differentiated by being set in bold type and the wide spacing between lines.

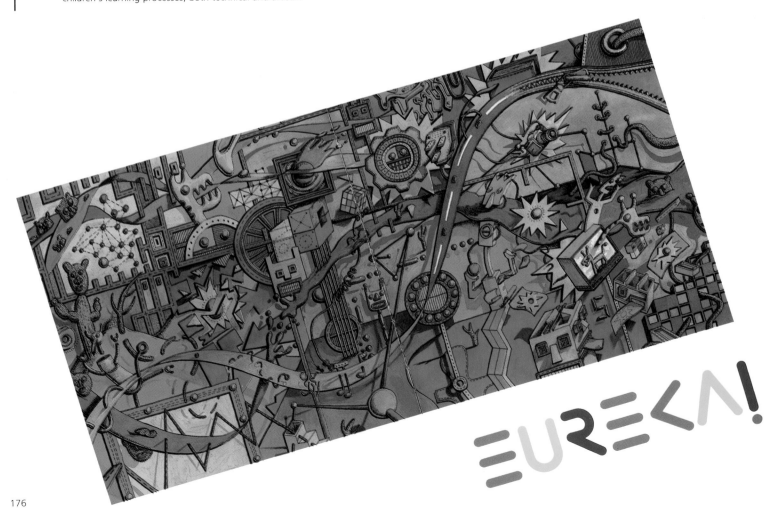

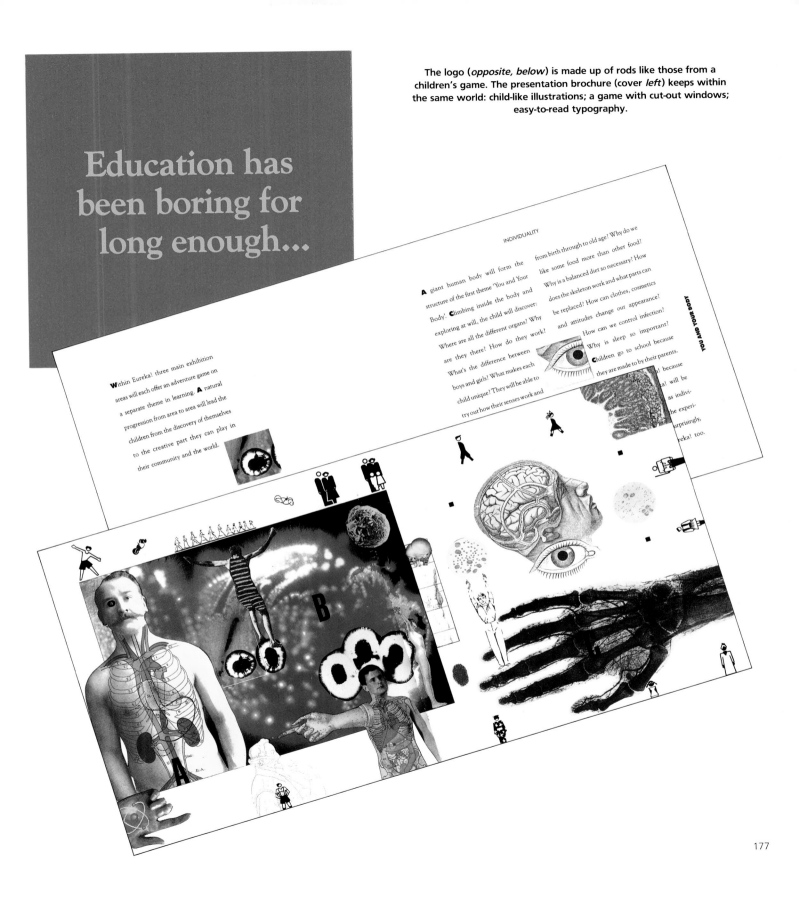

The logo (*opposite, below*) is made up of rods like those from a children's game. The presentation brochure (cover *left*) keeps within the same world: child-like illustrations; a game with cut-out windows; easy-to-read typography.

Education has been boring for long enough...

Within Eureka! three main exhibition areas will each offer an adventure game on a separate theme in learning. A natural progression from area to area will lead the children from the discovery of themselves to the creative part they can play in their community and the world.

INDIVIDUALITY

A giant human body will form the structure of the first theme 'You and Your Body'. **C**limbing inside the body and exploring at will, the child will discover: Where are all the different organs? Why are they there? How do they work? What's the difference between boys and girls? What makes each child unique? They will be able to try out how their senses work and from birth through to old age? Why do we like some food more than other food? Why is a balanced diet so necessary? How does the skeleton work and what parts can be replaced? How can clothes, cosmetics and attitudes change our appearance? How can we control infection? Why is sleep so important? **C**hildren go to school because they are made to by their parents.

YOU AND YOUR BODY

177

Designers' biographies

Addison Design Consultants

112 East 31st Street, New York, NY 10016, USA

Tel. (1) 212 532 6166; fax (1) 212 532 3288

Alan Peckolick   P. 44

Peckolick (b. 1940) graduated from the Pratt Institute (1961). In 1964, he became Herb Lubalin's assistant. He was chosen as one of the best young American designers by Gallery 303, New York (1967). In 1968 he opened his own studio. He rejoined Lubalin as vice president and creative director (1972), was an executive of Lubalin Peckolick Associates until 1982, Pushpin Lubalin Peckolick until 1985 and the Pushpin Group until 1986, when he founded Peckolick + Partners. Then (1989) he became director of Addison New York, part of Addison Design Consultants. He is famous for his elegant typographic designs, used by corporations worldwide for logos, posters, packaging, annual reports, corporate identity, etc. His work has been widely exhibited in the US and abroad and is in the permanent collection of the Gutenberg Museum, Mainz.

Roland Aeschlimann   Pp. 153–55

Grand Théâtre de Genève, 11 boulevard du théâtre, 1211 Geneva 11, Switzerland

Tel. (41) 22 21 23 18; fax (41) 22 29 49 19

Aeschlimann (b. Switzerland) studied under Hans Hartmann in Berne and Emil Ruder, Max Schmid and Armin Hofmann in Basel. He worked for Geigy (Basel, 1959–63), then as an art director in Osaka, Japan (1963–65). From 1965–66 he was on Josef Müller-Brockmann's team in Zurich and Nuremberg. He then worked as a designer, including exhibitions, for Geigy in Basel (1966–74). Since 1974 he has been a freelance set designer for theatres and numerous opera houses, e.g. in Geneva, Zurich, Bonn, Hanover. He collaborated with Herbert von Karajan on an Easter Salzburg Festival project. He designed programme layouts and posters for the Geneva opera (1976–80). Since 1980 he has designed numerous posters for Le Cabinet des Estampes, Geneva; the Musée des Beaux-Arts, Berne; and the University of Cologne. In 1991 he was invited to give masterclasses at the University of Quebec, Montreal. He has designed books for the Whitney Museum, New York.

Asaba Design Co. Ltd

3–9–2 Minami-Aoyama, Minato-ku, Tokyo 107, Japan

Tel. (81) 3 3479 0471; fax (81) 3 3402 0694

Katsumi Asaba   Pp. 123–25

Asaba was born in 1940 in Yokohama. After graduating from the design department of Kanagawa Prefectural Technical High School (1958), he worked in a department store before attending the Kuwazawa Design School, Tokyo. He joined the Keinosuke Sato Typography Research Institute (1961), then moved to Light Publicity (1964). In 1975 he founded Asaba Design Co. Ltd. Major clients include Seibu Department stores, Takeda Chemical Industries and the Nissan Motor Company. He has recently been involved with 'Typography: a view from Tokyo' at the Cooper Union School of Art, New York (1990), and 'Close-up of Japan – Kuala Lumpur 1991', a Malaysian exhibition of Japanese

Graphic Design. Among the professional associations of which he is a member is the Tokyo Art Directors Club. His graphic design, advertising and film commercials have won several awards, including the Mainichi Design Prize.

Les Ateliers du Nord

Place du Nord 2, 1005 Lausanne, Switzerland

Tel. (41) 21 20 58 07; fax (41) 21 20 58 43

Antoine Cahen and Claude Frossard   Pp. 153–55

Frossard (b. Ardon, Switzerland, 1947) trained as an architectural draughtsman, then studied industrial design in Lausanne. He worked as an industrial designer in Karachi (1976–79), before travelling in Asia. In 1983 he set up Les Ateliers du Nord with Antoine Cahen and Werner Jeker. Cahen (b. Lausanne, 1950) trained in industrial design at the Ecole Cantonale des Beaux-Arts et d'Art Appliqué, Lausanne (1971–75), then worked freelance (1975–83).

Les Ateliers du Nord specializes in industrial design for clients, as well as designing and producing items under the label ADN Design. Among its clients are Logitech (computer hardware); Swatch (watches); and the Musée Suisse du Jeu. It has created sign systems for hospitals and other public buildings. Exhibitions of its work include 'Les Ateliers du Nord, studio de design et graphisme' (Villeurbanne, France, 1990).

Flo Bayley   Pp. 157–59

74 Fentiman Road, London SW8 1LA, England

Tel. (44) 71 735 1512; fax (44) 71 793 1104

Flo Bayley (b. 1954) studied graphic design at the London College of Printing. She joined Conran Associates (1977), where her projects included a corporate identity for Next and repackaging the Mothercare range. She created the identity of the Boilerhouse Project at the Victoria & Albert Museum (1981), and designed catalogues and posters for it, including *Coke!*, which *The Face* described as helping to make it 'the most successful gallery of the '80s'. Since 1984 Flo Bayley has run her own graphic design and retail consultancy. Her clients include Paperchase and Penhaligon's. She has illustrated Antonio Carluccio's cookbooks; designed posters for the South Bank Centre; and created a corporate identity and labelling system for the Design Museum. Her designs are characterized by a witty pragmatism. She is fastidious about typography and clarity, believing that too many designers indulge themselves at the clients' expense. She says, 'Sound thinking beforehand saves expense later; this is a principle too few designers understand.'

Burns, Connacher & Waldron, Design Associates Inc.

59 West 19th Street, Suite 4a, New York, NY 10011, USA

Tel. (1) 212 255 5542; fax (1) 212 255 9156

Alan Hopfensperger   Pp. 36–37

Hopfensperger (b. Ohio, 1963) graduated from the University of Cincinnati's College of Design, Architecture, Art and Planning *summa cum laude*. At Vignelli Associates in New York, he worked on corporate identity and other projects for clients like the Children's Museum of Manhattan, the Guggenheim Museum and DuPont. He is now with Burns, Connacher & Waldron. His work on the Children's Museum logo won several awards (1989), e.g. *Communication Arts'* Award of Excellence; a silver award from the Art Directors Club. The Capital Campaign Invitation and Press Kit also won prizes, e.g. from AIGA (1988/89). Hopfensperger's work has been most strongly formed by the Swiss

Design associations

AIGA The American Institute of Graphic Arts

1059 Third Avenue, New York, NY 10021, USA

Tel. (1) 212 752 0813

The Graphic Artists Guild

11 West 20th Street, New York, NY 10011, USA

Tel. (1) 212 463 7730

ICOGRADA (International Council of Graphic Design Associations)

PO Box 398, London W11 4UG, England

Tel. (44) 71 603 8494

ICOM (Conseil International des Musées)

1 rue Miollis, 75015 Paris, France

Tel. (33) 1 47 83 77 81

Magazines and reviews

BAT

96 rue du faubourg Poissonnière, 75010 Paris, France

Tel. (33) 1 42 85 30 88

Blueprint

26 Cramer Street, London W1M 3HE, England

Tel. (44) 71 486 7419

Collector

45 rue Sedaine, 75011 Paris, France

Tel. (33) 1 43 57 52 05

Creation

Recruit Co. Ltd, 8–4–17 Ginza, Cho-ku, Tokyo 104, Japan

Tel. (81) 3 3575 1111

Design Quarterly

Walker Art Center, Vineland Place, Minneapolis, MN 55403, USA

Tel. (1) 612 375 7600

Eye

26 Cramer Street, London W1M 3HE, England

Tel. (44) 71 486 7419

Graphis

107 Dufourstrasse, CH 8008 Zurich, Switzerland

Tel. (41) 1 38 382 11

HQ (High Quality)

Maximilianstrasse 31, D-8000 Munich 22, Germany

Tel. (49) 89 22 9197

Linea Grafica

49 Via della Moscova, 2021 Milan, Italy

Tel. (39) 2 655 2498

Novum

Verlag F. Bruckmann KG, Nynphenbrigerstrasse, 8000 Munich 20, Germany

Tel. (49) 89 1 25 73 22

Print

104 Fifth Avenue, New York, NY 10011, USA

Tel. (1) 212 463 0600

Photographic credits

References are to page numbers, followed by position on the page.
Key: l = left, r = right, t = top, b = bottom.

Addison Design Consultants 44. **Philippe Apeloig** 85. **ARCO** 147, 149. **Cato Design** 50, 51, 53, 54, 55. **CCI, Paris** 120. **Centre Georges Pompidou, Paris** 78. **Chermayeff & Geismar Associates** 17, 20, 21, 22, 32, 33. **Roman Cieslewicz** 75, 76. **Communication Visuelle/Sophie and Roger Pfund** 154 t, 155. **Studio Dumbar** 25 tr, 131, 136, 137, 138, 139, 140, 141. **Emery Vincent Associates** 47, 48, 49. **Lorraine Ferguson** 23, 24. **Milton Glaser** 39. **Grapus** 66, 69. **Gregotti Associati** 114, 115, 117, 118, 119. **Hard Werken Design** 98 l, 132. **Ernst Hiestand** 107 tl, 107 bl.

Igarashi Studio 10 b, 41. **Italo Lupi** 31 b, 116, 121. **Mendell & Oberer** 94, 95, 96, 97. **Minale, Tattersfield & Partners** 168, 169. **Musée du Louvre** 63. **Pentagram** 30, 31 t, 45, 160r, 161 tr, 162, 166, 167, 172, 173, 174, 175. **Projekt Design** 93. **Pushpin Group** 8, 14. **Günter Ranbow** 10 t. **Stedelijk Museum, Amsterdam/Tjeerd Frederikse** 133; **Stedelijk Museum** 9. © **Fundació Antoni Tàpies** 144 tl, 144 br, 145 l, 145 r (Raimon Ramis). **Barrie Tucker Design Pty Ltd** 52. **Vignelli Associates** 14 t, 34, 35 b, 36, 37, 38. **Visual Design/Bruno K. Wiese** 105 t, 105 b. **Visuel Design** 76, 77, 82, 83, 84, 86, 87, 105 l. **Walker Art Center, Minneapolis** 25 l, 25 br, 26, 27. **Westpoint Design Consultants** 170. **Kijuro Yahagi** 128, 129. **Zéro 2/Nicolas Girard** 107 tr, 107 br.

Author and publisher wish to acknowledge the generous help of museums and designers in providing photographic material, and apologise for any inadvertent omissions from this list.